The Christian's Identity in a Lost World

210 325-354

Ashly

The Christian's Identity in a Lost World

A BIBLICAL LOOK AT IDENTITY

Dr. Ashley Maurice Mayhon

To order copies of this work and others contact:

By Email
ashmayhonrn@yahoo.com
preachsoundoctrine@yahoo.com

Reply on:
preachsoundoctrine.com

ISBN-13: 9780692928967
ISBN-10: 0692928960

preachsounddoctrine.com

Acknowledgments

I FIRST THANK GOD, THE Father, Son and Holy Spirit for saving me and working though me to accomplish this work. Without His grace I would not have had the Spirit, heart, understanding, time, opportunity, patience, or endurance to complete this work.

Thank you Lord, for your glory.

I thank all who have prayed, encouraged and supported me in my service to the Lord.

I give special thanks to my lovely wife Amber for her patience and encouragement, for she has sacrificed tremendously for me and ultimately for God in patiently long suffering and supporting me throughout the years of my ministry.

I thank my daughter Ashley and dedicate this book to her and my other children, walk in the Lord even if it cost you everything.

Contents

Acknowledgments · vii
Identity in a Lost World · · · · · · · · · · · · · · · · · xi

Part: 1 Knowledge of God · · · · · · · · · · · · · · · · · 1
Part: 2 Knowledge of Self · · · · · · · · · · · · · · · · ·17
Part: 3 Identity in Christ · · · · · · · · · · · · · · · · · 67

Works Cited · 99

Identity in a Lost World

MANKIND HAS AN IDENTITY PROBLEM. *Identity* is "a condition or a characteristic of who or what a person or thing is; qualities and beliefs that distinguish or identify that person or thing from others; the state of being" (*Dictionary*, 2017). Evidence of this identity problem can be seen in man's continual search for identity in material possessions. The American culture is permeated with the idea that material possessions give identity.

Dr. Ryan T. Howell (2014), an assistant professor at San Francisco State University and a contributing author in *Psychology Today* writes:

> *Multiple studies show that materialists, compared to non-materialists, have lower social and personal well-being. Compulsive and impulsive spending, increased debt, decreased savings, depression, social anxiety, decreased subjective well-being, less psychological need satisfaction, and other undesirable outcomes have all*

been linked with materialistic values and materialistic purchasing behaviors (Para. 1).

Materialism and similar behaviors are nothing new for Jesus commanded men to guard against such temptations over 2000 years ago: "*...Watch out! Be on your guard against all kinds of greed; life does not consist in an abundance of possessions*" (Luke 12:15 New International Version). The person who chooses to ignore this mandate will inevitably be drawn into the "deceitfulness of wealth," thinking materialism will produce happiness and fulfillment (Mark 4:19). Many seeking their identity through the pursuit of material possessions have wandered from what is right (the faith) and have pierced themselves with many sorrows (1 Timothy 6:10).

Man naturally seeks for identity outside of himself for he was not created to find identity in himself but in God, his Creator. In observing man's desire for identity, some men have exploited other men by tempting them with material possessions for their benefit. In fact, the *New York Times* points out that the U.S. economy is predominantly driven by consumer spending, which comprises approximately 70 percent of all U.S. economic growth and, "*if consumers are to continue to drive the economy, they must be in a sound financial position; if they become overburdened with debt, they are not able to maintain their position as the primary driver of economic growth*" (Stewart, 2010, Para. 1).

In other words, manufacturers and those who have a vested interest in driving the economy are to keep consumers right at the breaking point without pushing them over the edge. Man will never have identity and lasting contentment until he is reconciled with and walks with his Creator, for the natural man is never satisfied (Proverbs 27:20).

Scripture reveals that Christ followers have dedicated their lives to Christ and not to consumerism, materialism, humanism or any other "ism" ideology or philosophy. In fact, they referred to Him as *Lord*, meaning "complete master," the authority in which they submitted and laid down their lives.

In the sixth chapter of Romans, the apostle Paul writes, *"But now that you have been set free from sin and have become slaves of God, the fruit you get leads to sanctification and its end, eternal life"* (v. 22 English Standard Version). Jesus did not simply pay the price for sinners and set them free to go their own way again; rather, He sets them free from the bonds of sin for His purpose of giving them identity. A *slave* as referred to in this context by the apostle was known to have received his identity from his master in the ancient world. Likewise, a father would also give identity to his offspring as referred to in Romans 8, which says, "... *you have received the Spirit of adoption as sons, by whom we cry, 'Abba! Father!'"* (v. 15 ESV). The apostle later adds how a believer should think of this new identity in everyday life:

> brothers and sisters, in view of God's mercy, [you are] to offer your bodies as a living sacrifice, holy and pleasing to God—this is your true and proper worship. Do not conform to the pattern of this world, but be transformed

by the renewing of your mind. Then you will be able to test and approve what God's will is—his good, pleasing and perfect will (Romans 12:1, 2 NIV).

This surrender and allegiance to Christ alone as a slave was never thought to be optional. Jesus told His followers in the Upper Room, *"You are my friends if you do what I command you"* (John 15:14 ESV) and prior to this command, He told a crowd: *"...If you abide in my word, you are truly my disciples, and you will know the truth, and the truth will set you free"* (John 8:31, 32 ESV). Jesus also directly says, *"If anyone serves me, he must follow me; and where I am, there will my servant be also. If anyone serves me, the Father will honor him"*(John 12:26 ESV) and *"...If anyone would come after me, let him deny himself and take up his cross daily and follow me"* (Luke 9:23 ESV).

The word "if" is used in all four verses: "if you" or "if anyone." This word "if" is used in these four verses to introduce a conditional clause. A conditional statement discusses known factors or hypothetical situations and their consequences (*Grammarly*, 2017). Logic uses a similar statement, which is symbolized by "p → q," also known as an "if-then" statement in which "p" is a hypothesis (premise), and "q" is the conclusion.

From Jesus' statements, the following principles can be determined:

1) **If** one is a true believer, **he will** abide in God's Word (Evidence—fruit).

2) **If** one is truly born of the Spirit, **he will** preserve holding to the teachings of Jesus.
3) **If** one is a true Christian, **he will** be obedient to Christ. (The test is true obedience.)
4) **If** one is to be obedient to Christ, **he must** deny self and surrender all (Romans 12:1).

When a person proclaimed to be a Christian in the ancient world, the fact that his self-identity was found in his Master, Lord, Deliverer and Purchaser was automatically assumed. Early Christians were urged to count the cost of following Christ (Luke 14:28). Great crowds followed Jesus, and He knew some were only there for the benefits—food, healing, entertainment. By advising His followers to count the cost, Jesus was instructing them to recognize the terms and conditions before following Him because that devotion would cost them all, including their identity.

In other words, a believer could not simply add Christ to his current life and lifestyle. A person could not follow both Christ and the world (Matthew 6:24). Christ was to be the center of the believer's life. For denying all to follow Him, some risked everything, including their very lives as they faced imprisonment and/or death (Philippians 1:21). Therefore, the proclamation of being a Christian was not simply a profession as is so often observed today; rather, it was an identity change received after a true profession of faith.

An identity change can be observed in the fact that, before redemption, men are described as being in darkness, alienated from God and needing reconciliation. After redemption, men are referred to by a number of passive designations, including "children of God," "children of light," "lights of the world," "salt," "members of the body of Christ" and "ambassadors for Christ." Not only are believers described in a passive sense, but they are also labeled in the active sense as "athletes"; "soldiers for Christ"; "branches that abide in the Vine"; and "babies that desire (long for) pure, spiritual milk (God's Word). These descriptions remain instrumental in helping believers understand their identity in Christ.

With many people, self-help programs, books and philosophies competing for the Christian's heart and mind, what is the Christian to do and trust? The Christian is to start and end with the Word of God. Though some may agree with this conclusion, they still feel that the Word of God does not address every given situation. God's Word may not appear to directly address every situation; however, God's Word does indeed cover every situation principally for the believer is told, *"When the Spirit of truth comes, he will guide you into all the truth..."* (John 16:13 ESV). Truth (God's Word) not being addressed in detail is not the issue; rather, it is the lack of or difficulty in articulating the truth revealed in detail similar to Romans chapter 8:

> *"Likewise the Spirit helps us in our weakness. For we do not know what to pray for as we ought, but the Spirit*

himself intercedes for us with groanings too deep for words. And he who searches hearts knows what is the mind of the Spirit, because the Spirit intercedes for the saints according to the will of God" (vv. 26, 27 ESV).

Man is without excuse for God has sufficiently given him everything he needs for life and growing in godliness (Romans 1:20, 2 Peter 1:3).

God speaks in two primary ways concerning all things, including identity, through His Word: *"And we have the prophetic word more fully confirmed, to which you will do well to pay attention as to a lamp shining in a dark place, until the day dawns and the morning star rises in your hearts* (2 Peter 1:19 ESV), and through His Spirit: *"But the anointing that you received from him abides in you, and you have no need that anyone should teach you. But as his anointing teaches you about everything, and is true, and is no lie—just as it has taught you, abide in him* (1 John 2:27).

Standard and Point of Reference While Seeking True Identity

The church has historically held the view that the Bible is infallible and inerrant. The Modern Age (the nineteenth and twentieth centuries), however, has given rise to a so-called higher criticism. Not only has this criticism attacked the inspiration of Scripture but also the concept of infallibility and inerrancy (Sproul, 2014, p. 30).

Jesus taught the inerrancy and infallibility of scripture in the following verses: *"For truly I tell you, until heaven and earth disappear, not the smallest letter, not the least stroke of a pen, will by any means disappear from the Law until everything is accomplished"* (Matthew 5:18 NIV), *"...Scripture cannot be broken—"* (John 10:35 ESV) and *"Sanctify them by the truth; your word is truth"* (John 17:17 NIV). If Scripture cannot fail, Scripture cannot error. To profess that the Bible is infallible is to profess that the Scriptures are incapable of teaching error.

The church has historically believed that all of the words in Scripture were God's Words, and that for one to believe and obey the Bible was to believe and obey God Himself (Allison, 2011, p. 79). Church tradition and authority played a role in the lives of believers but was always viewed as subservient to Scripture (the Bible). The truth is that church tradition and authority has always been subservient to Scripture, for if it were the other way around, the church would simply be following man's ideas, fantasies and opinions.

The church has historically recognized the Bible as having been written in such a way that its teachings are able to be understood by all who read its truths, as long as they seek God's help and willingly follow its teachings (right heart, intent with the help and guidance of the Holy Spirit). The Bible has been written in such a way that both ordinary believers and biblical scholars are able to understand it rightly. Furthermore, the church has acknowledged that some parts of the Bible are quite puzzling and even difficult to understand. The formula adopted by the early church for understanding obscure portions of Scripture was to understand or interpret obscure passages in light of obvious portions of scripture (Allison, 2011, p. 120).

THE NEED FOR WISE COUNSEL

Scholars, theologians and scientists of the twentieth and twenty-first century are not perfect; rather, they have perfected the ideas of earlier generations, avoiding the same mistakes and failures while improving on their ideas, leading to success. This process has led the present generation to unthinkable heights, though certainly, the observation should be noted that every generation has made mistakes, has weathered setbacks and is less than perfect. Therefore, this current generation can also look forward to mistakes and avoid many by not being wise in their own eyes and embracing honesty.

The fact that this generation is not yet history must be realized as the final word has not been written. While taking into account that no generation is perfect, one would do well to remember the instruction of Proverbs 12:15 (ESV): *"The way of a fool is right in his own eyes, but a wise man* [or generation in this case] *listens to advice."*

One of the most troubling observations about the current generation is that many so-called scholars have been caught falsifying documents and evidence in order to advance their agenda rather than letting the evidence speak. At other times when the evidence is present, there is simply a failure to acknowledge what does not correspond to one's presupposition (Romans 1:28).

Every human being must admit that he has at least one bias (if not many); if not, that person is perfect. If one acknowledges this fallen human flaw, he would be wise to actively resist such destructive bias that will distort his perception, causing self-deception and the misrepresentation of information (Jeremiah 17:9).

Guarding against biases and misrepresentations requires a diligent search of the Scriptures to see if what the current teachers are advocating is true (Acts 17:11). For, *"Where there is no guidance the people fall, but in abundance of counselors there is victory"* (Proverbs 11:14 New King James Version) and *"Without counsel plans fail, but with many advisers they succeed"* (Proverbs 15:22 ESV).

WISE COUNSEL IN THE HISTORIC CHURCH

From the perspective of wise counsel, the Westminster and London Baptist 1689 Confessions are concise, biblically objective and considered by many to be the best systematic theological statements ever recorded. Dating back nearly 350 years, the Westminster Confession and the London Baptist confessions have stood the test of time.

THE WESTMINSTER CONFESSION

The Westminster Confession (c. 1640) was drafted and approved by over 150 of the world's most prominent Reformed theologians. The document originated from a need of the Protestant churches to lay a formal foundation of doctrinal guidelines for the church (Reformed Protestant Churches of England and those to come around the world).

As a result, the Puritan parliament called a church synod at Westminster. A *synod* is "an ecclesiastical governing, governing assembly and/or advisory council" (*Merriam-Webster*, 2017). The resulting document was *The Westminster Confession of Faith*. A *confession* is "a skillfully and highly influential set of biblical doctrines drafted from the Bible and categorized and systematized for congregational understanding." *The Westminster Confession of Faith* is considered by many to be the best statement of systematic theology ever framed by the Christian church (*gotquestions.org*, 2017).

As an attempt to "correctly handle the word of truth" (2 Timothy 2:15), *The Westminster Confession of Faith* is said to have accomplished this goal for nearly 400 years, remaining the primary Biblical doctrinal standard for Protestant and evangelical churches around the world (*gotquestions.org*, 2017). Several other denominations, including Baptists and Congregationalists, have used adaptations of *The Westminster Confession of Faith* as a basis for their own doctrinal statements. In each case, the Westminster

Confession is subordinate to the Bible (*gotquestions.org*, 2017).

THE LONDON BAPTIST CONFESSION

The 1689 *London Baptist Confession of Faith* was written by Calvinistic Baptists in England to set forth a formal expression (with a Baptist perspective) of the Reformed and Protestant Christian faith (*Theopedia*, 2017). The 1689 *London Baptist Confession of Faith*, like *The Westminster Confession of Faith* (1646) and *The Savoy Declaration* (1658), was written by evangelical Puritans who were concerned with their particular church organization reflecting what they perceived to be Biblical (*Theopedia*, 2017). "The 1689 Confession, alongside the Westminster Confession and Savoy Declaration, are considered to be the most important reformed confessions made in the English-speaking world" (*Theopedia*, 2017).

THE CONFESSION'S EFFECT ON AMERICA

Particular Baptists developed churches in colonial America, and in 1707, the Philadelphia Baptist Association was formed. These Baptists were called "Particular" because they held to the Calvinistic particular view of the atonement (*Theopedia*, 2017). The Philadelphia Baptist association formally adopted the 1689 confession in 1742 after it was endorsed by individual churches and congregational members. The Baptist Confession was then renamed *The Philadelphia Confession of Faith.* Furthermore, the Calvinistic Baptist Church Association formed in the mid-to-late eighteenth century and adopted the confession as *The Baptist Confession* (*Theopedia*, 2017).

MAN AND PURPOSE

One's true identity can be seen in his purpose. Everything created has both a particular purpose and a general purpose. The general and overall purpose is always for the glory of God: *"For from him and through him and to him are all things. To him be glory forever. Amen"* (Romans 11:36 ESV) and *"yet for us there is one God, the Father, from whom are all things and for whom we exist, and one Lord, Jesus Christ, through whom are all things and through whom we exist"* (1 Corinthians 8:6 ESV).

In particular, each individual will bring glory to God in a unique way through his gifts and talents, while all of creation will bring glory to Him in general. Nothing created or in existence is without purpose for, if it exists, it is by the will of God (Proverb 16:4). To claim that God, in His omniscience and omnipotence, would make or will that something exist that has no purpose would be irrational, if not blasphemous, for scripture throughout reveals God active even down to detail.

God has an ultimate purpose for all creation and every individual. Man's individual acts have know effect on God's overarching purpose and plan that is being ful-filled: "*The Lord has made everything for its purpose, even the wicked for the day of trouble*" (Proverbs 16:4 ESV). Every created thing serves a purpose. Even that which is invisible, such as angels and immutable laws regarding sound waves, gravity and oxygen, serves a purpose. These laws are stable, allowing man to use them for a purpose.

Man from the Beginning
In the first chapter of the Bible, Genesis 1, the Bible reads, "*So God created man in his own image, in the image of God he created him; male and female he created them*" (v. 27 ESV).

At one moment man was not; the next moment, man was brought into existence. God had the ability to create man anyway He desired for He had the power, right and ability. God chose to make man in His image.

God made all things—earth and everything that man would need to accomplish the task given him. After God created everything necessary, He created man and gave him dominion over these things. God's creation was very good (Genesis 1:31). The Bible reveals the God of all creation, power and dominion gave some of His power and dominion without necessity to a being He created (Adam particularly, and mankind in general).

God created everything that man would need; then He created him in His image with a purpose already known from all eternity, for nothing is new in God. If something were new to God, He would have new knowledge, making

Him ignorant of something, and therefore, not omniscient. Man did not have to wait for purpose; rather, purpose was already present before man was created. Therefore, God takes out the guesswork; man is without excuse, and His purpose for existence is clear (Romans 1:20).

Next, God placed man within a set parameter:

> "*The LORD God took the man and put him in the garden of Eden to work it and keep it. And the LORD God commanded the man, saying, 'You may surely eat of every tree of the garden, but of the tree of the knowledge of good and evil you shall not eat, for in the day that you eat of it you shall surely die*' " (Genesis 2:15-17 ESV).

These verses not only establish right, wrong and consequences for right and wrong, but the passage also reveals man's limitations. Man is not totally free to do what he wants; rather, he is bound by the rules of God. Man has freedom and the ability to perform his God-given task within the framework that God has established.

Genesis chapter two (v. 16, specifically) and the beginning of chapter three reveals that, with the power vested in man for good, he was still able to do evil and disobey. This capacity reveals that the good given by God can and often is used for evil. After the Fall, the great wickedness of man is revealed: "*The LORD saw that the wickedness of man was great in the earth, and that every intention of the thoughts of his heart was only evil continually*" (Genesis 6:5 ESV).

Lastly, the Bible reveals that even creation suffered consequences at the hand of man (Adam's disobedience). The ground was cursed, and thorns and thistles came forth. Under the inspiration of the Holy Spirit, the apostle Paul wrote, *"that the creation itself will be set free from its bondage to corruption and obtain the freedom of the glory of the children of God. For we know that the whole creation has been groaning together in the pains of childbirth until now"* (Romans 8:21, 22 ESV).

Man has no power or true identity outside of God for He is the Creator, establishing purpose for the creature; the Source, giving power and dominion to the creature; and the Sustainer, holding all things together for the creature to act.

Man's Acts Under the Sovereignty of God

Man's minor finite purpose falls under God's sovereign and immutable purpose. God has always had a purpose before the foundation of the world: *"even as he chose us in him before the foundation of the world..."* (Ephesians 1:4 ESV). Since man's purpose falls under God's overarching sovereign and immutable purpose, God's purpose must be understood first in order to understand man's purpose.

The word *providence* is not found in Scripture; nevertheless, the word has traditionally been used to summarize God's ongoing relationship with His creation (Grudem,

1994, p. 315). God's *providence* can be defined as "God's being continually involved with His creation in such a way that He is the very key to its existence." God maintains the properties in which He created and directs their distinctive properties to cause them to function as they do to fulfill His purpose (Grudem, 1994, p. 315). The interrelation of providence can be seen in verses such as Hebrews 1:3, where it is written: Christ is "upholding the universe by his Word of power" or in Colossians 1:17 (ESV), which says, *"And he is before all things, and in him all things hold together."*

God's holding all things together, preserving and sustaining them is not that difficult for most to grasp; however, one may wonder how is his actions meaningful and consequential if God is sovereignly over all things and working them out for His purpose and glory. The Bible presents God's sovereignty, providence and man's free choice as parallel concepts and does not reconcile them. Therefore man has no right to attempt to reconcile them. Man is accountable for his actions and God is sovereign over all.

GOD'S SOVEREIGNTY AND MAN'S CHOICES WORKING TOGETHER

God has given man purpose, duty and the ability to carry out his purpose and duty. After God gave man purpose and ability, He informed him that He would have uninterrupted communion (fellowship) with Him if he obeyed (reward). If, however, man chose not to obey, he would then experience separation along with death (punishment) if he did not: "...*for in the day that you eat of it you shall surely die*" (Genesis 2:17 ESV). This verse shows that man's actions are meaningful and consequential.

The Bible reveals that man's acts after the fall are not neutral, and God is absolutely sovereign: "*The LORD saw that the wickedness of man was great in the earth, and that every intention of the thoughts of his heart was only evil continually*" (Genesis 6:5 ESV). Man's slant is biased toward evil.

"*For since the creation of the world God's invisible qualities— his eternal power and divine nature—have been clearly seen, being understood from what has been made, so that people are without excuse*" (Romans 1:20 NIV). Man's decisions are meaningful and hold consequences.

According to the following verses, God is absolutely sovereign: "*declaring the end from the beginning and from ancient times things not yet done, saying, 'My counsel shall stand, and I will accomplish all my purpose'*" (Isaiah 46:10 ESV). "*Many are the plans in the mind of a man, but it is the purpose of the LORD that will stand*" (Proverbs 19:21 ESV).

God's sovereignty can be thought of as God's orchestrating everything—placing every individual where He wants the person to be (location), knowing perfectly what, when and how that would act (omniscience); thus accomplishing what He desired to accomplished in that moment for His ultimate glory and the good of the believer (Romans 8:28).

The believer, the unbelieving, the righteous, and even the unrighteous serve a purpose: *"The* L ORD *hath made all things for himself: yea, even the wicked for the day of evil"* (Proverbs 16:4 NKJV).

Purpose can be seen in the life of Egypt's Pharaoh's as well: *"But, indeed, for this reason* [purpose] *I have allowed you to remain, in order to show you **My power** and in order to proclaim **My name** through all the earth"* (Exodus 9:16 New American Standard Bible).

The free-sovereignty connection can be understood best by how the apostle Paul's following explanation: *"But **by the grace of God** I am what I am, and his grace toward me was not in vain. On the contrary, **I worked harder** than any of them, though it was not I, but the grace of God that is with me"* (1 Corinthians 15:10 ESV).

The early church confessed and understood the creation of man with a purpose as,

> After God had made all other creatures, He created man, male and female with reasonable and immortal souls, endued with knowledge, righteousness, and true holiness, after His own image; having the law of God written in their hearts, and power to fulfill it; and yet under a possibility of transgressing, being left to the liberty of their own will, which was subject unto change. Beside this law written in their hearts, they received a command, not to eat of the tree of the knowledge of good and evil; which while they kept, they were

happy in their communion with God, and had dominion over the creatures (*The Westminster Confession*, 2017, Ch. IV. Sec. II).

The church also understood man's free will as it related to God's overarching purpose and sovereignty:

I.   God has endued the will of man with that natural liberty, that is neither forced, nor, by any absolute necessity of nature, determined good, or evil.

II. Man, in his state of innocency, had freedom, and power to will and to do that which was good and well pleasing to God; but yet, mutably, so that he might fall from it.

III. Man, by his fall into a state of sin, has wholly lost all ability of will to any spiritual good accompanying salvation: so as, a natural man, being altogether averse from that good, and dead in sin, is not able, by his own strength, to convert himself, or to prepare himself thereunto.

IV. When God converts a sinner, and translates him into the state of grace, He frees him from his natural bondage under sin; and, by His grace alone, enables him freely to will and to do that which is spiritually good; yet so, as that by reason of his remaining corruption, he does not perfectly, or only, will that which is good, but does also will that which is evil.

V. The will of man is made perfectly and immutably free to do good alone in the state of glory only (*The Westminster Confession*, 2017, Ch. IX).

God is revealed in scripture as saving undeserving man (sinners) in the midst of their free will (sins) as explained in Colossians 1:13 (ESV), which says, *"He has delivered us from the domain of darkness and transferred us to the kingdom of his beloved Son,"* and in John 8:36, *"So if the Son sets you free, you will be free indeed"*.

The early church understood salvation to be from God in His grace and grace alone, for God's grace is necessary. Man could not help or restore himself to a right relationship with God; if he could, Christ would not have ever come (Colossians 2:13).

After the fall of man's federal head Adam, a change occurred in the heart of man that rendered him helplessly in bondage and inclined to sin, bound by the corruption of his sinful nature (Romans 5:19). As a result, man is prone to sin, does indeed sin, and thus is responsible for his sin.

The unmerited favor of God (sovereign grace) is defended by the apostle Paul when he reasons with those in Rome, writing, *"Has the potter no right over the clay, to make out of the same lump one vessel for honorable use and another for dishonorable use?"* (Romans 9:21 ESV).

Part 1: Knowledge of God

GOD'S PURPOSE

THERE ARE LIMITS TO A person's knowledge of God, like there are limits to everything as it relates to man's abilities. Man is finite and has no absolute knowledge of anything; *"The secret things belong to the LORD our God, but the things that are revealed belong to us and to our children forever, that we may do all the words of this law"* (Deuteronomy 29:29). A person's limited knowledge and finite understanding of the Infinite does not mean that he does not have true or meaningful knowledge of God. Man's knowledge concerning God is also limited because God has not revealed everything about Himself and His intentions to man (Sproul, 2014, p. 71).

Boyce (1887) characterizes God's will as referring to the power inherent in His nature by which He purposes and chooses the existence and the end of all things. An all-powerful, absolutely independent God, who is controlled by and dependent upon nothing, must will, in which He determines His own actions (Boyce, 1887). God's will does not give existence to Himself (as a being) nor does it make His nature what it is; on the contrary, God wills because He exists and has a nature.

The will of God is made known through nature (natural revelation), mutual love, relationships, creation, providential laws, mechanical and physical arrangements, mechanisms and actions. God wills what and whom He will create as well as the times, places and circumstances in which He will place those creatures in His creation. Therefore, He marks out the paths for His creatures. They are created for His purpose. He gives them the power and ability to choose; however, their will in choosing remains subordinate to His will. Their actions are under His control for He controls all circumstances and could stop them if He so desired. Man's thoughts and actions flow from and are influenced by his nature; so is the case with God. However, the difference is that God is simplistic. In other words, God is not composed of parts. This understanding or doctrine is often referred to as "Divine simplicity." The understanding is that God is identical to His "attributes" (characteristics): omnipresence, omniscience, omnipotent, omniscient, goodness, truth, eternity, and they are not qualities that make up His being nor are they abstract entities inhering in God as in a substance.

God does not will what He cannot accomplish, and His will is always best. God is perfect; therefore, He is immutable and never changes His will. If He did, His will would be based on new knowledge or information (as if He were ignorant at one point in time). God also sovereignly controls all events and is able to do all things because He possesses all power (omnipotence).

In contemplating the will and purpose of God, the following words of Jesus should be considered: "*...It is not for you to know times or seasons that the Father has fixed by His own authority*" (Acts 1:7 ESV). Under the inspiration of the Holy Spirit, the wisest man who ever lived wrote: "*It is the glory of God to conceal a matter, But the glory of kings is to search out a matter*" (Proverbs 25:2 NASB).

In pursuit of identity, it is helpful to distinguish between the decretive and preceptive will of God. The *decretive will* is "the will of God by which He purposes or decrees," while the *preceptive will* of God is "the will of God which He prescribes to others to be done," such as keeping His laws and statutes. The decretive will is always fulfilled; the preceptive will may be disobeyed, and therefore remain unfulfilled. The purpose of God is immutable, and His will cannot be resisted for He: "*declaring the end from the beginning and from ancient times things not yet done, saying, 'My counsel shall stand, and I will accomplish all my purpose,'*" (Isaiah 46:10 ESV). A rhetorical question is also asked in Romans chapter nine: "*For who is able to resist his will*" (Romans 9:19 NIV) Of course, no one can resist the will of God. Consequently, since God's will cannot be resisted, He will surely perfect that which He intends. His will is not contingent or dependent on anyone or anything (Boyce, 1887, p. 97).

The decretive will is sometimes referred to as God's absolute will, the sovereign will of God or the efficacious will of God. Again, when God sovereignly decrees that something should come to pass, it must indeed come to pass (Sproul, 2014, pp. 71-72).

One clear example of God's decretive will in scripture is the decree to crucify His Son. God is seen to have decreed that His Son should die on a cross in Jerusalem at a particular time in history, and indeed, His will on sending His Son to the cross came to pass in that place, at that time and in that manner (Sproul, 2014, pp. 71-72).

The following are a few prophetic verses supporting the decree of Christ's crucifixion: Psalm 41:9 (ESV) refers to Judas Iscariot and the part he played in the crucifixion story: *"Even my close friend in whom I trusted, who ate my bread, has lifted his heel against me."* Zechariah 13:7 (NKJV) prophesies the Lord's being forsaken by His disciples: *"Awake, O sword, against My Shepherd, and against the Man who is my companion,' says the LORD of hosts. 'Strike the Shepherd [Jesus], and the sheep shall be scattered...."* Mark 14:50 (ESV) fulfills Zechariah's prophecy: *"And they all left him and fled."* Zechariah 11:13 (ESV) mentions the betrayal money Judas was paid: *"...So I took the thirty pieces of silver and threw them into the house of the LORD, to the potter."* The prophecy was fulfilled in Matthew 27:7 (ESV), *"So they took counsel and bought with them the potter's field as a burial place for strangers."*

The preceptive will of God, on the other hand, is unlike the decretive will of God in that it can and is often resisted. The preceptive will deals with laws, commandments and duties under which God places His creatures and instructs them to fulfill. In others words, it is the rule of duty (Boyce, 1887, p. 97). Nonetheless, when God's laws/decrees are violated, they do not often carry an immediate consequence.

Distinguishing the decretive will of God from the preceptive will of God to understand one's true identity is helpful; however, the decretive will and the preceptive will of God should never be divorced for they are both the will of God, and He still renders consequences. Therefore, a person may have the God-given power (ability) to disobey God's law and duty, but he does not have the power to annul or terminate the consequences that follow for God's will is still ultimate.

God's decrees or the things He has willed (determined), which are just, wise, holy, perfect and eternally pure originating within Himself (Boyce, 1887, p. 97). Since God formed His decrees, they must have His character. The fullness of God's purpose cannot be totally comprehended by any created being for created beings are finite. Man not only has to deal with this finite ability and God's not revealing all to him, but he also has to cope with his corrupted flesh.

Since man battles with the flesh, lives in a world that is dominated by the flesh and is in constant conflict with the forces of darkness, he must intentionally deny his flesh and seek divine guidance continually (the Word in the Spirit). Special revelation is only possible by the power of the Holy

Spirit, in which man can see his perfect identity in Christ through His perfect justice, wisdom and holy perfection (John 1:12, Ephesians 1:5).

THE DECREE OF GOD FROM A HISTORICAL PERSPECTIVE

Over four hundred years ago Bible experts (theologians) believed the following:

> God from all eternity, did, by the most wise and holy counsel of His own will, freely, and unchangeably ordain whatsoever comes to pass; yet so, as thereby neither is God the author of sin, nor is violence offered to the will of the creatures; nor is the liberty or contingency of second causes taken away, but rather established (*The Westminster Confession*, 2017, Chapter III Sect. I).

This belief and understanding is supported from scripture in that the eternal, holy, wise counsel of God can be seen in the following verses:

Ephesians 1:11 (King James Bible), *"In whom also we have obtained an inheritance, being predestinated according to the purpose of him who worketh all things after the counsel of his own will."*

Romans 9:15 (KJV), *"For he saith to Moses, I will have mercy on whom I will have mercy, and I will have compassion on whom I will have compassion."*

Hebrew 6:17 (KJV), *"Wherein God, willing more abundantly to shew unto the heirs of promise the immutability of his counsel, confirmed it by an oath."*

While God is the all-powerful ruler and orchestrator of all, He is never to be blamed for sin, evil or temptation (James 1:13). In spite of how things may appear, we are told that, *"Every good gift and every perfect gift is from above, coming down from the Father of lights, with whom there is no variation or shadow due to change"*(James 1:16 ESV). *"And we know that for those who love God all things work together for good, for those who are called according to his purpose"* (Romans 8:28 ESV).

In Light of the Baptist Confession

The Baptist theologians of 1689 expressed similar convictions in their confession as follows:

> God hath decreed in himself, from all eternity, by the most wise and holy counsel of his own will, freely and unchangeably, all things, whatsoever comes to pass; yet so as thereby is God neither the author of sin nor hath fellowship with any therein; nor is violence offered to the will of the creature, nor yet is the liberty or contingency of second causes taken away, but rather established; in which appears his wisdom in disposing all things, and power and faithfulness in accomplishing his decree (*The Baptist Confession*, Revised June 1996, Chapter XIII).

While the Baptists used similar text proofs to support their position, they also add a few Old Testament proofs that are not contained in *The Westminster Confession* such as the following: Isaiah 46:10 (ESV), *"declaring the end from the beginning and from ancient times things not yet done, saying, 'My counsel shall stand, and I will accomplish all my purpose.'"* Numbers 23:19 (ESV) *"God is not man, that he should lie, or a son of man, that he should change his mind. Has he said, and will he not do it? Or has he spoken, and will he not fulfill it?"*

DEDUCTION

Beings act, and God is the ultimate Being; therefore, He acts, wills and decrees. God could not be who He is without forming purposes and decrees. God's plans and purposes have existed from all eternity within Himself; that is, His immutable, omniscient and omnipotent plans depend on or wait for consult from no one (Isaiah 46:10, Psalm 33:11, Proverbs 19:21). The plan to carry out His purposes includes all things whatsoever will come to pass—not some things, but all things; not all things in general, but all things in particular (Proverbs 16:4, 1 Peter 2:8). God has absolute control over all things, including identity. God's knowledge is perfect in that it flows from His decrees. Unless, that is, one thinks God is simply a spectator watching and hoping that man will overcome all of the opposition of the world, the flesh and the Devil in his own power (Ephesians 2:3, 1 John 2:16). With such a view of the sovereign decree of God, one should not bother to pray, for God cannot intervene or help.

IN THE IMAGE OF GOD, BUT NOT GOD

Human beings are quite different from God. Besides being created, God does not bestow certain attributes or characteristics for it is impossible. In other words, God cannot create another God for it would not be another God; it would be a created being. It is an impossibility to communicate or transfer over certain attributes of God. Attributes that are impossible to transfer to another being are often referred to as "incommunicable attributes." God is identified as God by these special attributes, and man is identified by the lack of these attributes. These attributes include God's unchangeableness compared to man's ever changing, and God's omniscience compared to man's limited knowledge. Mankind is mortal—not divine.

Distinct names (used more so in the Old Testament) were a description of the identity or reflected a true characteristic of God (Grudem, 1994, p. 158). These names should not be confused with the communicable attributes of man, for these names were taken from human experience or emotion in order to describe parts of God's character. In other words, these names for God tell us something true about the identity of God (Grudem, 1994, p. 158).

Also, man is not identified with God in the moral sense for God is holy, and man is sinful. Man is in the image of God in the unique sense that man processes rational personality, intellect, emotion, and will, meaning he is able to think, feel and choose like God. Unlike man however, Jesus Christ is in the perfect, absolute image of God. Jesus did not become the image of God at the incarnation; rather, He has always been God from all eternity. He was born of a woman to take on human flesh (Colossians 1:15); therefore, Jesus is 100-percent God and 100-percent man.

IDENTITY SEEN IN MAN'S AIM

Man's goal in short is to follow the admonition of I Samuel 12:24 (ESV), which says, *"...fear the LORD and serve him faithfully with all your heart"* and Ecclesiastes 12:13 (ESV), *"...Fear God and keep his commandments, for this is the whole duty of man."*

God's will is for believers to be shaped in the image and likeness of His Son, Jesus Christ. This *shaping* or molding is referred to as "sanctification." Related to the word *saint*, which literally means "to be set apart or declared holy," *sanctification* is "a state of separation unto God." Jesus, in fact, prayed that God the Father would, *"Sanctify them* [His chosen ones] *in the truth; your word is truth"* (John 17:17 ESV). The will of God is that every believer be sanctified: *"It is God's will that you should be sanctified..."* (I Thessalonians 4:3 NIV).

Sanctification takes place after justification; however, unlike justification, it is a progressive work that continues throughout the believer's life. If one is truly justified he will be sanctified for God does not do one without the other. Unlike justification, which is an immediate work of God, sanctification is an undertaking that God continuously works out in the believer's life.

Sanctification is often confused with justification, which is a one-time legal declaration, were the believer is identified as *just* for God declares him to be just upon faith in Jesus Christ alone (Grudem, 1994, p. 725). Justification is taught in scripture as a separate work from sanctification, which can be observed in these few verses of Romans and Galatians:

> *"For by works of the law no human being will be justified in his sight, since through the law comes knowledge of sin"* (Romans 3:20 ESV), *"For we maintain that a man is justified by faith apart from works of the Law"* (Romans 3:28 NASB), and *"yet we know that a person is not justified by works of the law but through faith in Jesus Christ, so we also have believed in Christ Jesus, in order to be justified by faith in Christ and not by works of the law, because by works of the law no one will be justified"* (Galatians 2:16 ESV).

The primary driving issue of the Protestant Reformation was the doctrine of justification. Martin Luther, the Protestant reformer, was saved when he realized the truth of justification by faith **alone,** and he overflowed with a newfound joy in the Gospel (Grudem, 1994, p. 722).

The early Protestant church was convinced of the difference between sanctification and justification in the life of the believer when their leaders derived the following from scripture:

They, who are once effectually called, and regenerated, having a new heart, and a new spirit created in them, are further sanctified, really and personally, through the virtue of Christ's death and resurrection, by His Word and Spirit dwelling in them: the dominion of the whole body of sin is destroyed, and the several lusts thereof are more and more weakened and mortified; and they more and more quickened and strengthened in all saving graces, to the practice of true holiness, without which no man shall see the Lord (The Westminster Confession, 2017, Chapter XIII sect. I).

The London Baptist held the identical belief in its London Baptist Confession of 1689 (*The Baptist Confession*, Revised June 1996, Chapter XIII).

The main scriptural support for this teaching is found in verses such as Romans 6:6 (ESV), which says, "*We know that our old self was crucified with him in order that the body of sin might be brought to nothing, so that we would no longer be enslaved to sin,*" and Acts 20:32 (ESV): "*And now I commend you to God and to the word of his grace, which is able to build you up and to give you the inheritance among all those who are sanctified.*" Believers are being built up or *sanctified* by the

Word of God into the image of Christ, therefore the old self is crucified and the chains are broken by the work of Christ and the believer is continuously being changed by the empowering of the Holy Spirit who sets the believer on a new course of direction.

IDENTITY AND INDIVIDUALITY

God has displayed Himself as a Creator of variety. The person who notices God's variety does not need to be an astronomer looking through a telescope to notice the uniqueness of the stars or a botanist with a magnifying glass to realize the variety of plants that God has freely chosen to create.

God is seen working supernaturally, redeeming men from every tongue and nation: *"After this I looked, and behold, a great multitude that no one could number, from every nation, from all tribes and peoples and languages, standing before the throne and before the Lamb, clothed in white robes, with palm branches in their hands"* (Revelation 7:9 ESV).

God, in His sovereignty, places men in a variety of places to accomplish His purpose. When the believer is redeemed, his personality is not changed. This can be seen in the personality in the human writers of scripture, yet scripture is the Word of God. The Holy Spirit uses Peter in his second letter to the church to explain it as follows: *"For no prophecy was ever produced by the will of man, but men spoke from God as they were carried along by the Holy Spirit"*

(2 Peter 1:21 ESV). Therefore, God moves men along by His Spirit for His purpose and for His glory while not erasing their personality, background and education.

Variety, which is obviously a part of God's plan, can also be seen in the bestowing of the different spiritual gifts. In spite of these gifts functioning in different ways and capacities, they serve a united and ultimate purpose for the building up of the body for the glory of God (Ephesians 4:12). Spiritual gifts in the broader sense is any ability that is empowered by the Holy Spirit and is used in the ministry of the church (Grudem, 1994, p. 1016).

IDENTITY, SPIRITUAL GIFTS AND SANCTIFICATION

Spiritual gifts are not separated from sanctification; every believer is in the process of sanctification, and every believer has at least one spiritual gift. With the use of the Word of God as the primary tool, the Holy Spirit operates as Jesus taught in John 17:17, sanctifying the believer in the truth, the Word of God.

The Spirit illumines the Word through which the believer is sanctified, refining the new identity according to the following passages:

> "*Do not be conformed to this world, but be **transformed** by the renewal of your mind, that by testing you may discern what is the will of God, what is good and acceptable and perfect*" (Romans 12:2 ESV).

"*That according to the riches of his glory he may grant you to be strengthened with **power through** his Spirit in your inner being*" (Ephesians 3:16 ESV).

"*For all who are **led by** the Spirit of God are sons of God*" (Romans 8:14 ESV).

"*The Spirit himself bears witness with our spirit **that we are** children of God*" (Romans 8:16 ESV).

Abiding in the Spirit to be built up and sanctified toward a greater sanctification (process) can be seen in Colossians 2 when the apostle Paul writes about being "*rooted and built up in him and established in the faith, just as you were taught, abounding in thanksgiving*" (v. 7 ESV). In other words, in His sovereignty God will furnish the opportunities, and the Holy Spirit will convict the heart, thereby sanctifying the believer.

The believer will be moved to associate with other brothers- and sisters-in-Christ who share the same identity and Spirit in Christ. Associating with and being a part of the physical body of Christ, i.e., a church, will develop Christian character (identity) in the believer. This part of the sanctification process is not only through both social and private prayer, the preaching of and hearing the Word, but also in discipline, mutual sympathy and in the aid or pouring into the lives of others what the Lord has poured into the believer's life both temporally and spiritually. Whatever pertains to sanctification must be connected with and rightly obtained from divine, inspired truth, the Word of God, for, "*knowing this first of all, that no prophecy of Scripture comes from someone's own interpretation"* (1 Peter 1:20 ESV). Rather, God interprets God: *"For who knows a person's thoughts except the spirit of that person, which is in him? So also no one comprehends the thoughts of God except the Spirit of God"* (1 Corinthians 2:11 ESV).

Spiritual gifts, which are bestowed by the Holy Spirit for the sanctification of His people, is the consolation of the Father's grace. Since these gifts are officially appointed, man cannot confer or increase in them. A person obtains his spiritual gifts by unmerited favor; therefore, his ministry is only to be in the framework and parameters laid out in the Bestower's Word and should never contradict it.

Another reason for this is that there is no greater and complete truth than the inspired truth of His Word: *"That the man of God may be perfect, throughly furnished unto all good works"* (2 Timothy 3:17 KJV). The Word of God is sufficient for life and godliness (2 Timothy 3:16). Therefore, believers exercising their spiritual gifts are none other than vehicles of grace. Believers are not, however, appointed as personal channels of access to God, givers of spiritual gifts or blessings (in the supernatural sense) as seen in the Catholic church.

Part 2: Knowledge of Self

§

THE DUTY AND ABILITY OF MAN

THE WHOLE DUTY OF MAN is to "...*Fear God, and keep his commandments...*" (Ecclesiastes 12:13 KJV). Man cannot fulfill this command on his own because of sinful flesh (corrupt nature):

1. "*The LORD saw that the wickedness of man was great in the earth, and that every intention of the thoughts of his heart was only evil continually*" (Genesis 6:5 ESV).
2. "*We have all become like one who is unclean, and all our righteous deeds are like a polluted garment. We all fade like a leaf, and our iniquities, like the wind, take us away*" (Isaiah 64:6 ESV).
3. "*The heart is deceitful above all things, and desperately sick; who can understand it?*" (Jeremiah 17:9 ESV).
4. "*Behold, I was brought forth in iniquity, and in sin did my mother conceive me*" (Psalm 51:5 ESV).
5. "*And you were dead in the trespasses and sins in which you once walked, following the course of this world,*

following the prince of the power of the air, the spirit that is now at work in the sons of disobedience—among whom we all once lived in the passions of our flesh, carrying out the desires of the body and the mind, and were by nature children of wrath, like the rest of mankind. But God, being rich in mercy, because of the great love with which he loved us, even when we were dead in our trespasses, made us alive together with Christ—by grace you have been saved—" (Ephesians 2:1-5 ESV).

6. *"Jesus answered them, "Truly, truly, I say to you, everyone who practices sin is a slave to sin"* (John 8:34 ESV).

7. *"The natural person does not accept the things of the Spirit of God, for they are folly to him, and he is not able to understand them because they are spiritually discerned"* (2 Corinthians 2:14 ESV).

8. *"All have turned aside; together they have become worthless; no one does good, not even one* (Romans 3:12, ESV).

9. *"When the disciples heard this, they were greatly astonished, saying, "Who then can be saved?" But Jesus looked at them and said, "With man this is impossible, but with God all things are possible"* (Matthew 19:25, 26 ESV).

10. *"That which is born of the flesh is flesh, and that which is is born of the Spirit is spirit. Do not be amazed that I said, 'You must be born again'"* (John 3:6, 7 NASB).

THE EFFECT OF SIN ON MAN'S IDENTITY

The first sin separated man from God, and his continual sin kept him hiding from God like Adam initially did when he had sinned: *"And they heard the sound of the LORD God walking in the garden in the cool of the day, and the man and his wife hid themselves from the presence of the LORD God among the trees of the garden"* (Genesis 3:8 ESV). Man inherited corruption from Adam because Adam represented mankind. This inheritance is similar to the inheritance that we receive from God through faith when one puts his faith in Jesus Christ. Jesus is the believers representative by faith like Adam was appointed by God to be man's representative. By nature when a person is born, he is born of the seed of sinful corrupted man and therefore sins. When a person puts his faith in Jesus, he is born again—not of corruptible seed but incorruptible; therefore, the believer receives all the benefits of Christ and will live forever (1 Peter 1:23).

Consequences like depravity, corruption and alienation are usually referred to as "original sin." The term, original sin, does not refer to the first sin in particular as the name may suppose; rather, the designation describes the *consequences* of the first sin. *Depravity* is a unique term, which refers to the lack of original righteousness or holy affection toward God (Sproul, 2014). Corruption of one's moral nature gives him a bias toward evil (sin) and therefore against God, his Creator and Identity Holder (Sproul, 2014).

With a depraved nature, a person can never know his true identity. Depravity with inability can be seen throughout the New Testament: *"dead in trespasses and sins"* (Ephesians 2:1), *"sold under sin"* (Romans 7:14), we are in *"captivity to the law of sin"* (Romans 7:23), and *"by nature children of wrath"* (Ephesians 2:3). These Scripture portions refer to a person who is powerless to find his true identity without divine intervention.

Every person has walked in the course of this world, lost and not knowing his identity, following the passions of his flesh and carrying out his own desires (Ephesians 2:2, 3). The natural corrupt man and the flesh is at enmity with God, desiring things opposed to God and nothing good comes from his flesh; therefore, identity is wholly from God (Romans 7:18, 8:7, Galatians 5:17).

In spite of this helpless, lost corrupted state, God, being rich in mercy and grace, took on the form of a Man to do what no other could do (Ephesians 4:10). *"For it is by grace you have been saved, through faith—and this is not from yourselves, it is the **gift** of God"* (Ephesians 2:8 NIV).

Only by the power of the Holy Spirit can a person be brought to life from death (depravity). God is the One who makes a person alive and gives him identity: *"For we are his workmanship, created in Christ Jesus for good works, which God prepared beforehand, that we should walk in them"* (Ephesians 2:10 ESV).

Mankind has always been dependent on God: *"And he is not served by human hands, as if he needed anything. Rather, he himself gives everyone life and breath and everything else"*

(Acts 17:25 NIV). Human beings are even dependent on God for what we often refer to as natural resources, for Jesus said, *"…He causes his sun to rise on the evil and the good, and sends rain on the righteous and the unrighteous"* (Matthew 5:45 NIV).

Man is physically and spiritually dependent on God. Man is unable to regain, restore, preserve or deliver himself to an adequate relationship with God.

MANKIND FAIL WITH THE FALL

The universal fallen nature can be seen in Romans 3:10 (NIV), which says, *"As it is written: 'There is no one righteous, not even one.'"* Jesus affirmed this fact in His conversation with the rich young ruler: *"Why do you call me good?…No one is good—except God alone"* (Mark 10:18 NIV). The Bible clearly states that there are no "good" people and even calls His creations *sinners*. *"On hearing this, Jesus said to them, "It is not the healthy who need a doctor, but the sick. I have not come to call the righteous, but sinners"* (Mark 2:17 NIV).

DESIRE WITHOUT THE ABILITY

Jesus redeems the believer; however, the believer has not experienced final glorification on this side of heaven and therefore struggles with sin, the flesh, and identity:

> *"I do not understand what I do. For what I want to do I do not do, but what I hate I do. And if I do what I do*

not want to do, I agree that the law is good. As it is, it is no longer I myself who do it, but it is sin living in me. For I know that good itself does not dwell in me, that is, in my sinful nature. For I have the desire to do what is good, but I cannot carry it out. For I do not do the good I want to do, but the evil I do not want to do—this I keep on doing. Now if I do what I do not want to do, it is no longer I who do it, but it is sin living in me that does it" (Romans 7:15-20 NIV).

This passage shows that the apostle Paul still struggled with sin and denying his flesh.

The Lord Jesus Christ said, *"Watch and pray that you may not enter into temptation. The spirit indeed is willing, but the flesh is weak"* (Matthew 26:41 ESV). At this point, the Lord said, *"The spirit indeed is willing, but the flesh is weak,"* and later, the Bible says, *"It is the Spirit who gives life; the flesh is no help at all..."* (John 6:63 ESV).

Paul was a redeemed man during this struggle for the unredeemed: *"But a natural man does not accept the things of the Spirit of God, for they are foolishness to him; and he cannot understand them, because they are spiritually appraised"* (1 Corinthians 2:14 NASB). *"The mind governed by the flesh is hostile to God; it does not submit to God's law, nor can it do so"* (Romans 8:7 NIV). In other words, the mind without the Spirit is a mind governed and held captive by the flesh. A mind governed and held captive by the flesh cannot serve God, for Jesus said, no one can serve two masters (Matthew 6:24, Luke 16:13).

Several passages stress that the mind governed, enslaved and held captive by the flesh (not born again, unredeemed) cannot serve God: *"They are darkened in their understanding and separated from the life of God because of the ignorance that is in them due to the hardening of their hearts"* (Ephesians 4:18 NIV). *"For we ourselves were once foolish, disobedient, led astray, slaves to various passions and pleasures, passing our days in malice and envy, hated by others and hating one another"* (Titus 3:3 ESV). *Enslavement* is "bondage." The word *slave* is derived from the Greek word *doulos*, which means "become slaves, enslaved, held in bondage, made a slave or under bondage" (*Biblehub*, 2016).

Sin and therefore struggles with sin is not uncommon for the believer. In John's first letter to the church, he writes: *"If we claim to be without sin, we deceive ourselves and the truth is not in us"* (1 John 1:8 NIV). The Bible is written to believers, who are in a daily struggle—a battle with the world, the flesh and the Devil (1 John 2:16). Believers are told, *"Therefore do not let sin reign in your mortal body so that you obey its evil desires"* (Romans 6:12 NIV). In others words the believer should not hold allegiance to sin, having it ruling his life, for it is Jesus's position to rule the believers life.

Sin is universal: *"for all have sinned and fall short of the glory of God"* (Romans 3:23 NIV). A habitual pattern of sin can be seen immediately following the Fall: Adam and Eve hid from God, Adam blamed Eve, Eve blamed the serpent, and their son Cain murdered his brother (Abel).

Therefore, the power to refrain from sinning must come from a supernatural Holy Spirit.

ABILITY

Understanding the believer's ability and dependence on God is essential in understanding "who" he is in Christ and who God created him to be (identity). Man's redemption, sanctification, and his gifts should be understood as gifts from God (grace) for His glory for the prophet Isaiah writes:

> "*I am the LORD; that is my name; my glory I give to no other, nor my praise to carved idols*" (42:8 ESV).
>
> God wants man to seek His glory: "*He who speaks from himself seeks his own glory; but He who is seeking the glory of the One who sent Him, He is true, and there is no unrighteousness in Him.*" (John 7:18 NASB).

A person's view of his ability has greater implications then he may realize, for if he believes he has the ability to come to God and save himself, he will not only be self-deceived and confused but will also lack thanksgiving, put his faith in himself and fail to give glorify God.

If a person thinks he has found his way to God, he will naturally conclude that he should be proud of himself for he has made the right choice; now he has to figure out his identity and purpose. This idea is from the flesh for man is commanded not to glory in man (the flesh) for all is God's, *"Therefore let no man glory in men. For all things are your's"* (1 Corinthians 3:21 KJV).

THE EXTENT OF THE FALL

Human nature was indeed impacted by the first sin; the Devil was correct. Man would be like God, knowing good and evil for God is good and man would become evil (Genesis 3:5). All man knew up to the point of the first sinful act was good. Man's desires after the fall came then from this effected nature of evil. All of man's desires before regeneration stem from this evil, sinful nature. This nature can be seen in what Jesus said in Matthew 12:33, *"Either make the tree good and its fruit good, or make the tree bad and its fruit bad, for the tree is known by its fruit"* (Matthew 12:33 ESV). Jesus' perfect work and sacrifice makes the tree good; therefore, the fruit will be good. In other words, man can only desire what is in his nature to desire. When he is regenerated (born again), his desires are different because his nature is different. This asseveration leads to the question: can man change his nature? Is it possible in his corrupted nature to desire this change? Divine revelation reveals the following answer: *"For the wages of sin is death, but the free gift of God is eternal life in Christ Jesus our Lord"* (Romans 6:23 ESV), and *"...the mind of the flesh is death, but the mind of the Spirit is life and peace"* (Romans 8:6 American Standard Version). Scripture reveals that every thought of man's heart was evil all of the time, and every good and perfect gift comes from God (Genesis 6:5, James 1:17). Salvation is the ultimate perfect gift.

The Bible proclaims that *"...people loved the darkness rather than the light because their works were evil"* (John 3:19 ESV). Everyone had evil works; everyone loved darkness. Man's nature is inclined to sin (Ephesians 2:2).

There are three major biblical positions when referring to man's nature and ability after the fall (before conversion). They have been labeled here "A," "B," and "C". These three positions are the three major biblical systems derived for understanding man's nature and ability, from a biblical perspective. At least two of these positions date back to over 1500 years.

Many from position A and all from position C hold to the doctrine of the total depravity of man. Which means they believe that human nature is thoroughly corrupt and sinful as a result of the Fall. They derive this concept from verses like Genesis 6:5 - that every intention of the thoughts of his heart was only evil continually.

Those in position A who do not hold to the doctrine of total depravity of mankind believe that man is sick or tainted by sin but not to the extent that he cannot turn from his sin and choose God. This group will be designated the "A-nt" group, a sub group that adheres to the overall beliefs of group A but do not hold to the total depravity of man; hence, "A-nt" = not totally depraved.

Group A believes and teaches that Christ's work of redemption, dying on the cross for sins, was to remove an obstacle, which is referred to as the "unsatisfied claims" of justice. These claims stood in the way of God's offering pardon to sinners as He desired to do. The prerequisite was that they would believe (Packer, 1990, p. 131).

In other words, Christ's work, life and death on the cross persuaded (induced) the Father to accept graciously what He (Jesus) had accomplished to satisfy the Father's justice. In so many words, the Cross was not a triune plan of God. God was at war with Himself in the sense that God's justice stood in the way of God's (Christ Jesus) pardoning sinners, which God (Christ) desired to do for them "if" they would believe. Adding the word "if" to their believing means that the work could have been in vain, making God dependent on man and ignorant, not knowing whether or not man would believe. Of worth noting is the fact that the scripture says, *"For God so loved the world, that he **gave** his only begotten Son, that whosoever believeth in him should not perish, but have everlasting life"* (John 3:16 KJV). Therefore, God the Father was involved in the decision for He **gave** up His Son to purchase sinners. God's not completing the work of salvation would also contradict Philippians 1:6 (ESV), which says, *"...he who **began** a good work in you will bring it to completion at the day of Jesus Christ."* Again, the Bible shows that God did indeed initiate the work His Son performed on the cross.

According to group A, redemption secured for God a right to make an offer (of salvation) but did not ensure that anyone would accept the offer because faith is man's work, not the grace of God. In other words, Christ's work created an opportunity for man to exercise saving faith in his own strength without divine intervention.

Group C, on the other hand, believes, affirms and teaches that Christ's work on the cross was an actual substitutionary work. Christ stood in the place of those who would believe and endured their penalty. As a result, believing sinners are reconciled back to God because Christ paid their penalty. The sinner's punishment was placed on Him; their past, present, and future sins were all paid for, and eternal life was secured for them (1 Peter 3:18; John 3:16).

Group C also believes that God chose certain sinners for the purpose of redemption, so that God could manifest His grace, power and majesty (John 6:37-39; 6:44; 10:28; 15:16), giving them a measure of faith (Romans 12:3), which would result in their salvation. As a result, none of them are able to boast because God has graciously saved them (Ephesians 2:9). So God did not merely make salvation possible; He obtained it for them.

Sovereignly Purposed and Given an Identity

Human ability and God's sovereign purpose can be further evaluated by looking at Romans 9:11-29. Before Isaac's twin sons were born and before they had done anything good or bad, God had sovereignly purposed their lives: "...

The older will serve the younger" (v. 12 ESV). *"...Jacob I loved, but Esau I hated"* (v. 13 ESV). God also has plans for each individual's life that are only known in part; nevertheless, man is responsible for his actions. That God would give grace to anyone (for He did not have to) is a blessing. In spite of man's guilt, God still gives him grace. True, all men do not receive the same measure of grace; however, all do receive grace: *"so that you may be sons of your Father who is in heaven. For he makes his sun rise on the evil and on the good, and sends rain on the just and on the unjust"* (Matthew 5:45 ESV). By grace man receives sun and rain for he does not deserve it, and if God so chose, He could immediately punish man for his sin.

This doctrine is not an easy one to accept. Paul immediately addresses objectives in verses 14-18. Verse 14 asks the question, *"...Is there injustice on God's part?"* and directly he answers, *"...By no means!"* In other words, these objectives may seem "wrong" to the fallen human heart; however, God sets the standards, and He administers grace to whomever He so wills. Now justice, on the other hand, does have to be administered for it is the *penalty* or "just wage" for an act (in this case, the sinful works committed).

In this regard, God told Moses: *"...I will have mercy on whom I have mercy, and I will have compassion on whom I have compassion"* (v. 15 ESV). He adds that these things aren't based on human will or effort but on God who has mercy (v. 16). The foundation of man's salvation is God's mercy.

The Bible opens with God's carrying out His sovereign, eternal plan, *"In the beginning, God created the heavens and the earth"* (Genesis 1:1 ESV). From all eternity, God has done what He pleased not being restricted or restrained by anyone or anything.

Scripture reveals that God takes counsel from no one: *For the Scripture says to Pharaoh, "For this very purpose I have raised you up, that I might show my power in you, and that my name might be proclaimed in all the earth"* (Romans 9:17 ESV). This verse not only reveals the apostle's literal interpretation and reverence for God's Word, but also God's purpose for bringing Pharaoh to power: for God to display His power.

God's purposes are accomplished through man's actions. Though Pharaoh acted willingly to accomplish what he wanted, at the same time, the ruler was serving God's purpose. Scripture tangibly verifies this statement: *"But for this purpose I have raised you up, to show you my power, so that my name may be proclaimed in all the earth"* (Exodus 9:16 ESV).

This verse shows that God actively raises people to power to display His perfect justice, making an example of them so that the whole world can see and know that God is the one true God. The Scripture does not say that Pharaoh simply rose to power or that God allowed Pharaoh to raise to a powerful position; rather, God actively raised Pharaoh to power for the purpose of displaying His power.

God's deliberate plan can also be clearly seen in the crucifixion of His Son as well: *"This man was handed over to you by God's deliberate plan and foreknowledge; and you, with the help of wicked men, put him to death by nailing him to the cross"* (Acts 2:23 NIV).

God plainly teaches throughout scripture that He has a purpose and plan for everyone and everything. In spite of man's limitations, biases and weakness, his responsibility is to know what the Lord has spoken and instructed.

GOD KNOWS WHAT YOU WOULD DO

God, being all knowing and with perfect understanding, created all things through Jesus and for Jesus, and He knows perfectly how they will function: *"For in him all things were created: things in heaven and on earth, visible and invisible, whether thrones or powers or rulers or authorities; all things have been created through him and for him"* (Colossians 1:16 NIV). *"All things"* include situations which are referred to by theologians as "God's providence." In short, "God's providence" refers to God not only supplying all things, but also arranging all things according to His plan for His glory. As previously mentioned, God's providence can be seen in the crucifixion of His Son for He perfectly orchestrated every detail to present His Son as a holy sacrifice before the world. This providence can also be seen in the sanctification of His children, building character and in the punishment of the wicked. God's providence can be seen in how He sovereignly places all people in their particular places for their appointed purpose.

With knowing every individual's character, nature, ability and understanding perfectly, God places them where He desires them, with the purpose that they will fulfill His will/purpose. God knows what every individual will do in every situation, exactly as He knew what Pharaoh would do if he were given power.

Proverbs 19 fine-tunes this concept for, *"Many are the plans in the mind of a man, but it is the purpose of the LORD that will stand"* (v. 21 ESV). As a result of individuals' doing what they will and desire within the framework God provides for them, God makes Himself known by displaying His attributes of power, grace, holiness, justice, goodness, love, jealousy, etc.).

GOD'S SOVEREIGN POWER OVER IDENTITY

God's sovereign power can be seen in that not only did He punish Pharaoh but also the disobedient Egyptians who followed him. Some may question why God was not gracious to the Egyptian people. Why didn't God send His Son to save them (Ephesians 2:3)? Well again God is gracious and patient to all people to some extent. Grace is not mandatory; rather, grace is a gift, and God does not have to give the same gift to everyone. All that can be elucidated from scripture is that saving the Egyptians was not a part of the plan of God (Romans 11:26).

"For this time I will send all my plagues on you yourself, and on your servants and your people, so that you may

know that there is none like me in all the earth. For by now I could have put out my hand and struck you and your people with pestilence, and you would have been cut off from the earth" (Exodus 9:14, 15 ESV).

God sent plagues on the Egyptians for their disobedience, wickedness and unbelief. At that time, Egypt was a flourishing nation and perhaps the most prosperous in the world. Only a few hundred years prior to the plagues and the Red Sea miracle, the Bible recorded: *"...all the earth came to Egypt to Joseph to buy grain, because the famine was severe over all the earth"* (Genesis 41:57 ESV). During this time of prosperity, God raised Pharaoh to power.

Who made the Egyptians prosperous (James 1:17)? Are blessings good? God's power was demonstrated on these people in both blessing and condemnation: He raised them to power blessing them with untold riches, and He brought them down, decimating the population for the wicked acts that they willfully preformed. The prophet Daniel verifies God's power: *"He changes times and seasons; **he removes kings and sets up kings**; he gives wisdom to the wise and knowledge to those who have understanding"* (2:21 ESV). Clearly, whatever authority or power Pharaoh or anyone else has (or had) came from the sovereign hand of God.

The apostle Paul teaches: *For the Scripture says to Pharaoh, "For this very purpose I have raised you up, that I might show my power in you, and that my name might be proclaimed in all the earth." So then he has mercy on whomever he wills, and he hardens whomever he wills*" (Romans 9:17, 18 ESV). This verse is not the apostle's opinion; rather, this verse is God's (Holy Spirit) teaching.

Again, God's sovereignty does not diminish human responsibility for Pharaoh willfully disobeyed God. God sovereignly chooses how each person will serve His purpose; however, human responsibility is not annulled for man chose to sin rather than repent.

God knows perfectly what a person will do and why down to the most minuscule detail; in fact, in Luke 12:6 and 7 (ESV) Jesus tells His own not to be afraid and comforts them by saying that nothing is forgotten by God: "... *And not one of them is forgotten before God. Why, even the hairs of your head are all numbered. Fear not; you are of more value than many sparrows.*" This extraordinary, supernatural detail should remove the fear that God does not know or that He is not concerned.

IDENTITY IN THE FUTURE

Has God told man what the world's identity will look like in the future? God warns of terrible times to come: "...*in the last days there will come times of difficulty. For people will be lovers of self, lovers of money, proud, arrogant, abusive, disobedient to their parents, ungrateful, unholy*" (2 Timothy 3:1, 2 ESV). People in the future will be identified as lovers of self, prideful, arrogant and abusive.

Loving self, in essence, is not improper; however, when that love exalts itself as being greater than God, man's

Creator, it is self-worship, which is addressed in Romans 1:25 (ESV): "...*they exchanged the truth about God for a lie and worshiped and served the creature rather than the Creator, who is blessed forever! Amen.*"

Arrogance is defined by *Merriam-Webster* as "an attitude of superiority manifested in a presumptuous manner." In other words, the arrogant person fails to realize who he truly is (a creator) and suffers for it, unlike the prudent who sees danger and hides himself (Proverbs 22:3).

Abuse is misuse. The misuse of that which God created for man's good and benefit is rampant today.

The subject of pride was addressed last, for all of these characteristics flow from a prideful heart. The pride that God hates exalts itself above Him, is self-righteous and has no room for God in its heart. This pride can be seen in the wicked heart of the Devil. Three "I's" can be seen before he fell: "*You said in your heart, 'I will ascend to heaven; above the stars of God I will set my throne on high; I will sit on the mount of assembly in the far reaches of the north*" (Isaiah 14:13 ESV).

These characteristics of Satan dominate our deteriorating world, and many find their identities in them. The Christian, on the other hand, does not for he knows that these things are opposed to God, deceptive and destructive evils that await God's judgment.

Take Comfort

The justice of God is not intended to scare, but rather to give warning, for He has promised to never leave or forsake the man who is found in Him (Christ Jesus) (Deuteronomy 31:6, Hebrews 13:5). God will carry out His perfect justice; the blood of the Lamb covers the believer. Take heart *"For God has not destined us for wrath, but to obtain salvation through our Lord Jesus Christ"* (1 Thessalonians 5:9 ESV).

"For my thoughts are not your thoughts, neither are your ways my ways, declares the LORD. *For as the heavens are higher than the earth, so are my ways higher than your ways and my thoughts than your thoughts"* (Isaiah 55:8, 9 ESV).

The believer in pursuit of identity can take comfort in knowing that, in spite of the unknown, Jesus promised: *"…I am with you always, to the end of the age"* (Matthew 28:20), *"for I am with you, and no one will attack you to harm you, for I have many in this city who are my people"* (Acts 18:10 ESV).

The latter verse is not only comforting in the sense that Jesus is with man, but He is also divinely orchestrating all things. This promise is amazing in the sense that when disaster strikes, another person can be present and be of no help; however, Jesus proclaims that He is divinely in control and will protect His child. This assurance comes with a guarantee, power and authority for no one can do harm to God's elect (Ephesians 1:4, 2 Thessalonians 2:13, 2 Timothy 1:9). Jesus says, *"I give them eternal life, and they will never perish, and no one will snatch them out of my hand"* (John 10:28 ESV).

KNOWING ALL THINGS IS GOD'S IDENTITY

If God did not know the future perfectly, He would not be all knowing; therefore, He would not be God. If God failed to know anything past, present or future, He would fail to be God. In order to guarantee anything, He would have to know all things, including the probabilities of all things. One would have to say that God does not technically make adjustments, for making adjustments would indicate that something was not going according to plan. According to Isaiah 14:24 (ESV), *"The LORD of hosts has sworn: "As I have planned, so shall it be, and as I have purposed, so shall it stand."*

On the contrary, those in group A believe that Jesus had to persuade His Father to accept something less than His justice demanded, indicating that there is or was some form of separation or disunity between Jesus and His Father's will and purpose. Scripture never teaches such a separation in God (Trinity). Embracing this concept would also make God mutable in that He could lower His standard and change His mind, which would raise another problem. If God could be persuaded to lower His standard, why wouldn't He simply eliminate His standard or make it obtainable (low enough) that His Son wouldn't have to come into the world, live, die and rise again?

Scripture actually teaches the opposite of group A's theory. Deuteronomy 6:4 affirms the unity of God: *"Hear, O Israel: The LORD our God, the LORD is one"* (Deuteronomy 6:4 NIV). God, the Holy Spirit, the Inspirer of Holy Scripture speaks of Himself as being one in the book of Romans as well: *"since God is one—who will justify the circumcised by faith and the uncircumcised through faith"* (Romans 3:30 ESV).

How could God be at war with Himself or within Himself and be productive? Jesus did not allude to any such separation in God when He said, *"I and the Father are one"* (John 10:30, ESV). Jesus is saying, "The Father and I are one; there is no division between us." The question is whether or not there can be separation with God. He is perfect. Division indicates change and/or imperfection. Holy Scripture plainly and clearly teaches that there is neither change nor imperfection in God. James even goes so far to say, *"You believe that God is one; you do well. Even the demons believe—and shudder"* (James 2:19 ESV).

Furthermore, group A teaches that the Father moved from a throne of justice to a throne of grace to make atonement possible. This concept is totally unsupported and unfounded in scripture. This teaching paints a picture again of God warring with or within Himself. If God cannot be in agreement with Himself, how can He keep the universe together? The atonement doesn't persuade or move God to love us. On the contrary, the atonement is an illustration of something that God had already decided in eternity because of His love for man (Ephesians 1:4). God is not a man that He can be persuaded. There is confusion within the ranks of this group, but God must never be thought to possess confusion or to be confused.

If man be partially depraved, tainted or sick, as some in A group insist, then man is capable on his own to come to God. However, if man saves himself, serves God and stays in fellowship with Him on his own, why is there a need for this so-called persuasion? No particular Bible verses are used by group A to support this claim of good merit or partial depravity.

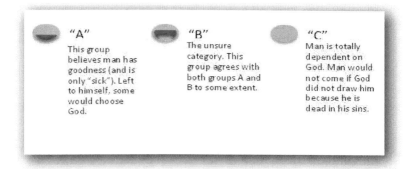

"A"
This group believes man has goodness (and is only "sick"). Left to himself, some would choose God.

"B"
The unsure category. This group agrees with both groups A and B to some extent.

"C"
Man is totally dependent on God. Man would not come if God did not draw him because he is dead in his sins.

"A"— is representative of Arminianism, which is based on the theological ideas of (Jacobus Arminius), a Dutch theologian (1560-1609).

"B"— represents the middle ground to which many adhere.

"C"— is representative of Calvinism, which is based on the Reformed theological ideas of John Calvin, the French theologian (1509-1564).

God's Glory in Salvation

God has said, *"I am the Lord; that is my name! I will not yield my glory to another or my praise to idols"* (Isaiah 42:8 NIV). If man could have saved himself, would God have sent His only Son? If sin could have been overlooked or paid for in any other way, would God not have allowed the cup to pass from His only begotten Son (Matthew 26:39, Luke 22:42)?

Jesus is necessary for eternal life: *"Jesus said to him, "I am the way, and the truth, and the life. No one comes to the Father except through me"* (John 14:6 ESV). This truth is throughout scripture; man's ultimate dependence is on God, not only for food, water and clothing as mentioned in Matthew 6 but also for faith, righteousness and eternal life.

THROUGH THE AGES

The standard Biblical doctrinal interpretation of the Protestant church has been that man became dead in sin after the Fall, and as a result, was wholly defiled in all the parts and faculties of soul and body (*The Westminster Confession*, 2017, Chapter VI:I, II).

Also, for the last nearly 400 years, the Protestant church has clearly documented and believed that Adam:

"being the root of all mankind, the guilt of this sin was imputed; and the same death in sin, and corrupted nature, conveyed to all their posterity descending from them by ordinary generation.

IV. From this original corruption, whereby we are utterly indisposed, disabled, and made opposite to all good, and wholly inclined to all evil, do proceed all actual transgressions.

V. This corruption of nature, during this life, does remain in those that are regenerated; and although it be, through Christ, pardoned, and mortified; yet both itself, and all the motions thereof, are truly and properly sin" (*The Westminster Confession*, 2017, Chapter VI: III-V.).

Therefore, "...*whoever is united* [identified] *with the Lord is one with him in spirit*" (1 Corinthians 6:17 NIV).

"*Now you are the body of Christ and individually members of it*" (1 Corinthians 12:27 ESV).

The world in which the believer lives is confused, blinded and led astray by the Enemy, and he wants to confuse and lead the believer astray as well. The believer can be lead astray by being kept ignorant. Nonetheless God's elect cannot be deceived: "*For false christs and false prophets will arise and perform great signs and wonders, so as to lead astray,* **if possible**, *even the elect*" (Matthew 24:24 ESV). Jesus said in John 8: "...*If you abide in my word, you are truly my disciples, and you will know the truth, and the truth will set you free*" (vv. 31, 32 ESV).

The Jews responded negatively however with human (fleshly) reasoning and hypocritical legalism like many do today: "...*We are offspring of Abraham and have never been enslaved to anyone...*" (v. 33 ESV). They were blinded by the Enemy and could not see their bondage. Today this legalism may come in the form of church membership, title or status.

Later, Jesus said, "...*I am the way, and the truth, and the life. No one comes to the Father except through me*"... (John 14:6 ESV) Therefore Jesus is man's guide to identity and out of this confusion. In fact the closing statement of *The London Baptist Confession 1689* reads:

> We the MINISTERS, and MESSENGERS of, and concerned for upwards of, one hundred BAPTIZED CHURCHES, in England and Wales (**denying Arminianism**), being met together in London, from the third of the seventh month to the eleventh of the same, 1689, to consider of some things that might be for the glory of God, and the good of these congregations, have thought meet (for the satisfaction of all other Christians that differ from us in the point of Baptism) to recommend to their perusal the confession of our faith, which confession we own, as containing the doctrine of our faith and practice, and do desire that the members of our churches respectively do furnish themselves therewith (*The Baptist Confession*, "Closing Statement and Signatories").

How Does Dependence Look?

How does this type of dependence look? If dependence is a part of a person's identity and if he fails to realize and live dependent on the Source as he was created to, then he will be operating from a false foundation. That false foundation, which would be most destructive, would only lead a person into deeper confusion and discontentment.

Dependence in the current culture is often viewed as negative for it implies the idea of one person's doing nothing while another does; therefore, dependence may be viewed as lazy. The *Merriam-Webster Dictionary* defines *dependent* as "the quality or state of being dependent; especially: the quality or state of being influenced or determined by or subject to another reliance, trust, one that is relied on." The dictionary definition of *dependence* being used to support this treatise is "trust and reliance," which is also supported by scripture. Man cannot do good for the glory of God without God, for in Him, man lives, moves and has his being; He holds all things together (Acts 17:28, Colossians 1:17).

The great Puritan theologian and philosopher, Jonathan Edwards, who is remembered for his sermon "Sinners in the Hands of an Angry God" and his part in sparking the Great Awakening, once said concerning man's dependence on God:

> "All the good that they have is in and through Christ; He is made unto us wisdom, righteousness, sanctification, and redemption. All the good of the fallen and redeemed creature is concerned in these four things, and cannot be better distributed than into them; but Christ is each of them to us, and we have none of them any otherwise than in him" (Edwards, 1731, Para. 5).

TRUST AND RELIANCE SEEN IN EARLY CHRISTIANS

The need for trust and reliance in God can be seen throughout the confessions. In its first chapter, the Westminster Confession says,

> "Although the light of nature, and the works of creation and providence do so far manifest the goodness, wisdom, and power of God, as to leave men inexcusable; yet are they not sufficient to give that knowledge of God, and of His will, which is necessary unto salvation. Therefore it pleased the Lord, at sundry times, and in divers manners, to reveal Himself, and to declare that His will unto His Church; and afterwards for the better preserving and propagating of the truth, and for the more sure establishment and comfort of the Church against the corruption of the flesh, and the malice of Satan and of the world, to commit the same wholly unto writing; **which makes the Holy Scripture to be most necessary; those former ways of God's revealing His will unto His people being now ceased**" (*Westminster Confession*, 2017, Chapter 1.1)

This excerpt shows the early churches' dependence, reliance and trust in God and particularly in His Word for guidance. An ultimate trust and reliance on the Lord to the end and in final judgment understood from scripture can be seen in the last chapter of *The Baptist Confession*:

> The end of God's appointing this day, **is for the manifestation of the glory of his mercy, in the eternal salvation of the elect;** and of his justice, in the eternal damnation of the reprobate, who are wicked and disobedient; for then shall the righteous go into everlasting life, and receive that fulness of joy and glory with everlasting rewards, in the presence of the Lord; but the wicked, who know not God, and obey not the gospel of Jesus Christ, shall be cast aside into everlasting torments, and punished with everlasting destruction, from the presence of the Lord, and from the glory of his power (*The Baptist Confession*, 1689, Chapter 32.2).

Dependence and reliance was what a slave or servant was expected to do. This can be seen in that the early church's hope for salvation was not in themselves; God's mercy manifested in Christ Jesus is referred to as "the eternal salvation of the elect" (Matthew 25:21-34, 46).

ONLY ONE OPTION

The only alternative to relying on the Spirit is relying on the flesh. "*It is the Spirit who gives life; the flesh is no help at all. The words that I have spoken to you are spirit and life*" (John 6:63 ESV). Man has only two options: Spirit or flesh.

The flesh always leads to sin. The believer's duty is to stay in the Spirit for the flesh is destructive. The Holy Spirit is not a force, an idea, or a mental mindset. Rather, the Spirit is God, the third person of the Trinity; the Spirit of God comes upon the believer and seals him when he is born again (John 3:7). Nicodemus inquired about this matter in the third chapter of the gospel of John where Jesus told Him: "...*Truly, truly, I say to you, unless one is born again he cannot see the kingdom of God... Unless one is born of water and the Spirit, he cannot enter the kingdom of God. That which is born of the flesh is flesh, and that which is born of the Spirit is spirit*" (3:3, 5, 6 ESV). In closing, Jesus adds that by believing in Him, a person will have eternal life (3:15).

Upon believing, that convert becomes a new creation, and old things are passed away (2 Corinthians 5:17). With new birth comes new desires and direction. With new desires come conflicts for that new believer still lives in the old, fallen human flesh. In the midst of these struggles, the Spirit of Truth leads (John 16:13), teaches (1 John 2:27), helps (Romans 8:26), intercedes in prayer (Romans 8:26) and searches all things (1 Corinthians 2:10). The Spirit of Truth reveals a person's true purpose and identity. Therefore, he cannot arrive at true purpose and identity without divine illumination. Hence, the believer cannot take credit for discovering his self; rather, he must give thanks to God for removing his heart of stone, opening blind eyes and revealing his true identity.

The Uselessness in Exploring Other Options

Knowing a solution for an identity crisis is useless if the person who is searching does not realize the extent of his need. Jesus informed the Jews of their need for Him, *"...It is not the healthy who need a doctor, but the sick. I have not come to call the righteous, but sinners to repentance"* (Luke 5:31, 32 NIV). When a man truly understands his sin, inability in the flesh to please God and his salvation and completeness in Christ ALONE, he will experience peace and true identity in addition to eternal life and all other blessings.

The Jews failed to realize their need for mercy and supernatural help to remove the blindness and pride. Being bound (enslaved) by sin, the Jews responded negatively and missed the cure (Jesus). Jesus explained to them that everyone who sins is a slave to sin and by being hypocritical with the law (legalism), they would perish in their sins. The Jews thought that their works: seeking after worthless things versus the Creator, going to the synagogue (Bible study/church), saying the right things, and even ethnicity, i.e., being descendants of Abraham would save them from the wrath of God. Jesus responded by saying, *"You search the Scriptures because you think that in them you have eternal life; and it is they that bear witness about me"* (John 5:39 ESV).

Sadly, many today hold similar views. In natural, human preconceived notions, people think they can figure out life and identity; however, there is nothing to resolve for the Word of God tells man who he is, how to live and where he is going. Believing in the Lord Jesus Christ is the way a person finds his true identity.

IF THE BONDAGE IS LIFTED, CAN MAN FIND HIS IDENTITY?

If a person repents and is born again, can he simply seek and find his identity? If bondage is removed, can man discover his identity without God? In the stronghold of enslavement, if that which kept a man bound were lifted, man could operate in only one of two ways: in the flesh or in the spirit. The apostle John opens his Gospel teaching that believers are *"children born not of natural descent, nor of human decision or a husband's will, but born of God"* (John 1:13, NIV). The new birth takes place by the action of the life-giving Spirit. Giving life implies that there was no life (death).

After regeneration, can man rise from his sickbed and find his way through the darkness? Paul says, *"For I know that nothing good dwells in me, that is, in my flesh. For I have the desire to do what is right, but not the ability to carry it out"* (Romans 7:18 ESV). Paul was in the situation to which he is referring: saved and set free; yet Paul still says he did not have the ability. What Paul meant is explained in the same verse. *"For I know that nothing good dwells in me, that is, in my flesh..."* (Romans 7:18 ESV).

When the Holy Spirit comes upon the believer, He is said to teach the believer all things, guiding him into all truth and speaking the authority of God (John 14:26;

16:23). The Spirit knows what and when to teach the believer (John 16:12). The flesh, on the other hand, cannot teach anything good for it is said not to be of any profit (John 6:63) and, *"For the flesh desires what is contrary to the Spirit, and the Spirit what is contrary to the flesh..."* (Galatians 5:17 NIV).

In addition, if a person was ever truly obedient unto true salvation in the first place, how could he be habitually disobedient to the leading of the Spirit now? The Spirit of God convicts of sin, leads the one committing the sin to repentance and gives him Godly desires, like trusting God at His Word.

The nature of the unredeemed individual, on the other hand, is set on the flesh; therefore, he is only inclined to sin, even though he may confess to the contrary. All the fleshly nature can do is sin to some lesser or greater extent, meaning that not all people sin to the same degree, and some people's sins are currently hidden. A sinful nature will always produce sin unless acted upon by the supernatural grace of God because the will is controlled by the nature. Hence, if the nature is fallen, everything—the thoughts, desires, motives, intentions, etc.—that follow after will fall.

Jesus said concerning the person who has been simply set free:

"When the unclean spirit has gone out of a person, it passes through waterless places seeking rest, and finding none it says, 'I will return to my house from which I

came.' And when it comes, it finds the house swept and put in order. Then it goes and brings seven other spirits more evil than itself, and they enter and dwell there. And the last state of that person is worse than the first" (Luke 11:24-26 ESV).

INDEPENDENCE HISTORICALLY

Can a person live out his identity apart from the power of God? Jesus created all things for Himself and for His purpose. Jesus holds all things together, and in Him we live, move and have our being; therefore, apart from Him nothing can be (Colossians 1:17; Acts 17:28). Nothing can truly exist apart from Him. When Colossians chapter one refers to *"all things,"* it means all things, including *all* life as well (v. 17).

Men can and often do fail to acknowledge God as God, claiming His nonexistence or impersonal nature. However, this claim is insincere for the apostle writes in Romans that men not only knew God but also knew that His character was righteous. Sinful men are said to suppress the truth of God with their unrighteousness (v. 18). It is not that truth could not be found; rather, the truth was suppressed by the sinner with ungodly desires (the love of darkness, John 3:19).

The suppression and hindering of the truth can be seen in the hostility of the militant atheist who fights against something that he claims does not exist. This hostility does not come from the person who truly and sincerely does not believe in the existence of God. Rather, it is from the one who knows God exists and is angry with Him because His character is contrary to his own, and He intrudes into his darkness with light. Instead of repenting, this person becomes ever more heartened, refusing to acknowledge His supremacy.

Not even thoughts escape or are independent of God. The early church not only believed this, but also believed that not even the fall was absent of God's presence:

> *The almighty power, unsearchable wisdom, and infinite goodness of God so far manifest themselves in His providence, that it extends itself **even to the first fall, and all other sins of angels and men**; and that not by a bare permission, but such as has joined with it a most wise and powerful bounding, and otherwise ordering, and governing of them, in a manifold dispensation, to His own holy ends; yet so, as the sinfulness thereof proceeds only from the creature, and not from God, who, being most holy and righteous, neither is nor can be the author or approver of sin (The Westminster Confession,* 2017, Chapter 5.4).

Scriptural support for this text is found in the following texts, which say,

> *"I will send him against an ungodly nation, And against the people of My wrath I will give him charge, To seize the spoil, to take the prey, And to tread them down like*

the mire of the streets. Yet he does not mean so, Nor does his heart think so; But it is in his heart to destroy, And cut off not a few nations" (Isaiah 10:6, 7 NKJV).

2 Samuel 24:1 (NIV), *"Again the anger of the LORD burned against Israel, and he incited David against them, saying, "Go and take a census of Israel and Judah."*

Acts 14:16 (KJV), *"Who in times past suffered all nations to walk in their own ways."*

Some are still said to be without strength in sin, carnal-minded in enmity against God and not subject to the law of God (Romans 5:6, 8:7). There is never an escape from the presence and power of God.

THE DESTRUCTIVENESS OF SIN ON IDENTITY

Sin is portrayed in the Bible as paralyzing and debilitating. God refers to man as being dead in sin and trespasses (Ephesians 2:1, Colossians 2:13). Seeing man's need for divine intervention is not difficult. Sin is an obstacle that not only keeps man from coming to God, but also keeps God from coming to man; as a result, man's identity is distorted (Sproul, 2014).

God loves man and desires to bless him, but sin interferes and God's perfect, righteous, holy disapproval rises up in justice instead. God is holy and righteous, and sin must be justly punished and condemned for this is perfect.

God is love; however, He is also holy, righteous and just. God's righteousness, love and justice can be seen in the outpouring of His wrath on His Son, for out of love, He had His Son take the sinner's place while He rightly and justly punished sin.

Judgment is always based on God's righteous nature. The God of love is hostile toward man because of sin (Romans 1:18). God can only come to man and man to God through the atoning work and sacrifice of His Son Jesus Christ.

At this point, some may wonder how God came to man in the Old Testament. Men put their faith in the Messiah, Jesus Christ, to come. Jesus was the promise spoken of right after the fall: *"I will put enmity between you and the woman, and between your offspring and her offspring; he shall bruise your head, and you shall bruise his heel"*(Genesis 3:15 ESV).

Therefore, man is propitious (favorable) because of Christ's work of atonement and His work ALONE, laying down His life in perfect obedience to reconcile mankind back to God (our Creator, Redeemer, Sustainer and **Identity Restorer**).

Matthew, in his account of the gospel, writes, *"And Jesus cried out again with a loud voice and yielded up his spirit. And behold, the curtain of the temple was torn in two, from top to bottom. And the earth shook, and the rocks were split"* (Matthew 27:50, 51 ESV).

The tearing of the veil dramatically symbolizes that the work of Christ was sufficient for the veil separated man from God and God from man. This four-inch-thick veil separated man from the Holy of Holies, the earthly dwelling place of God's presence. The veil was torn, giving man access to God. Christ's sacrifice makes possible for the worst individuals to approach God's throne of grace and therefore discover true identity (Hebrews 8:13; 10:19-20).

Man begins to realize reconciliation when the Holy Spirit convicts him of sin, and he finally sees God's abhorrence toward sin in a way that he never did before and repents. God's Word is then realized and honored as God's Word, and the believer is convinced of God's divine righteousness.

Sin is not a simple, single, isolated act; rather, it extends to every part of man's nature: mind, body, soul, will and emotions. No part of man is immune or protected from sin, which is why man could never simply come to God on His own or stay in God on his own, for *"Jesus replied, 'Very, truly I tell you, no one can see the kingdom of God unless they are born again"* (John 3:3, NIV). *Born again* in this verse refers to being born of Spirit, regenerated, having a new heart, becoming a new creation. If a man cannot see the kingdom of God without being born again, how much more so to seek it or enter it?

CAN GOD RESPOND TO SIN ANOTHER WAY?
God has to respond to sin in the way He does for His nature is holy and perfect. For God to respond to sin in

any other way is impossible, for He would be going against His own nature, which is impossible. For God to ignore His nature is impossible. Sin is an attack against God's being (His holy nature) for if sin could destroy God, it would; for by sin's very nature, it is destructive. If God did not punish sin, He would not only be unjust but also destroying or defeating Himself because ignoring sin is contrary to Him. Sin is the opposite of good and perfect.

Sin, by its nature, is irrational. This irrational nature can be seen in that man is naturally hostile toward his God, who is his only source of help, strength and freedom. However, sin is all man has ever known. Man loves his sin and cannot imagine life without it; therefore, he is naturally opposed to the one true God even though he may profess Him (John 3:19). The sinner sees no sin in God; rather, he sees the opposite and knows he has to make a choice. God's standards stem from His holy nature. Basically, God has six basic moral attributes: holiness, justice (righteousness), perfection, jealousy, goodness (love), and truth. Looking carefully at God's attitudes will present a better sense of who God is.

How Does Sin Look from God's Point of View?

With God, there are no small sins. People commonly dismiss sin that they consider minor or insignificant by justifying it and saying, "God forgives" or "He loves unconditionally." Such a judgment is idolatrous, for making any sin light or insignificant is not true of the one and only true God. God does love mankind; however, He cannot tolerate sin. God is perfect; therefore, He must judge sin perfectly.

The Israelites were guilty of dismissing sin and creating an idol for themselves shortly after they were delivered from bondage in Egypt. The Israelites knew the one and only true God and saw His power manifested firsthand against their enemies:

> *When the people saw that Moses delayed to come down from the mountain, the people gathered themselves together to Aaron and said to him, "Up, make us gods who shall go before us. As for this Moses, the man who brought us up out of the land of Egypt, we do not know what has become of him." So Aaron said to them, "Take off the rings of gold that are in the ears of your wives, your sons, and your daughters, and bring them to me." So all the people took off the rings of gold that were in their ears and brought them to Aaron. And he received the gold from their hand and fashioned it with a graving tool and made a golden calf. And they said, "These are your gods, O Israel, who brought you up out of the land of Egypt!"* (Exodus 32:1-4 ESV).

Despite the command not to worship idols and seeing the miraculous power God manifested before their very eyes, the children of Israel still followed the natural pattern of man, adopting false religions and worshiping of idols (Exodus 32:8). Even though God had delivered Israel from the bondage of Egypt, the people still turned to idols to lead them: "...*gods who shall go before us*" (v. 1) rather than looking to the one true God to lead them. The Israelites wanted a god with whom they could be more comfortable—a god that would tolerate their sin.

God, in His mercy and grace, did not turn His back on them even though He said to Moses, "...*I have seen this people, and behold, it is a stiff-necked people. Now therefore let me alone, that my wrath may burn hot against them and I may consume them, in order that I may make a great nation of you*" (Exodus 32:9, 10 ESV).

At other times, however, God does administer judgment even though the recipients may be unaware. "*Therefore God sends them a strong delusion, so that they may believe what is false, in order that all may be condemned who did not believe the truth but had pleasure in unrighteousness*" (2 Thessalonians 2:11, 12 ESV).

UNDERSTANDING GOD TO UNDERSTAND ONE'S IDENTITY
GOD'S HOLINESS

God's primary attribute is holiness. Some may have believed the primary attitude of God is love because of its frequent mention or the very fact that John penned under the inspiration of the Holy Spirit, "...*God is love*" (1 John 4:8). But holiness surpasses love in that God's love flows from His holiness. True, God's love is like none other; however, without holiness God's love would not be what it is. Holiness is not to be viewed as one attribute among others, but rather the sparkling representation of His perfection and His total glory.

Holiness refers to God's greatness, transcendent majesty, superiority, reverence and His virtue, which is worthy of honor. God is referred to in scriptures as being holy in nature as well as in character. The love of God flows from His holiness like other attributes. The Hebrew word for *holy* is *godesh*, meaning "apartness, otherness or sacredness." When saying "God is holy," attention is being called to note the difference between Him and all creatures. His love is apart or other then other creatures' love for God's love is supreme and passes understanding.

"*There is none holy like the LORD: for there is none besides you; there is no rock like our God*" (1 Samuel 2:2 ESV). The Greek word for *holy* is *hosios*, which means "righteous, holy or pious." From the moral stance, God is holy, and He is entirely separate from evil. God is holy in His very nature (Exodus 15:11). The question is asked in Exodus 15:11 (NIV): "*Who among the gods is like you, LORD? Who is like you—majestic in holiness, awesome in glory, working wonders?*"

The answer to this question is found in Leviticus 11:44, 45 (ESV), which says: "*For I am the LORD your God. Consecrate yourselves therefore, and be holy, for I am holy. You shall not defile yourselves with any swarming thing that crawls on the ground. For I am the LORD who brought you up out of the land of Egypt to be your God. You shall therefore be holy, for I am holy."* First Samuel 6:20 (NIV) mentions the complete inability of anyone's standing in God's presence because He is so holy: *And the people of Beth Shemesh asked, "Who can stand in the presence of the LORD, this Holy God? To whom will the ark go up from here?"*

God's holiness is pictured in Revelation 4:8 (ESV), which says: *And the four living creatures, each of them with six wings, are full of eyes all around and within, and day and night they never cease to say, "Holy, holy, holy, is the Lord God Almighty, who was and is and is to come!"* God's moral nature cannot allow anything less than holiness. God's standard is absolute holiness (Geisler, 2011). Mankind is absolutely hopeless without Jesus.

JUST

God is just (righteous). To be *just* is "to be totally right all of the time." In God's justice, He never punishes people unjustly or more than they deserve; He executes to them exactly what they deserve. Psalm 92 affirms that there is no wickedness within Him. The righteousness of God involves His righteous ordinances: *"…The ordinances of the LORD are true, and righteous altogether."* (Psalm 19:9 Revised Standard Version). God's throne is established on righteousness. Psalm 89:14 (NIV): *"Righteousness and justice are the foundation of your throne; love and faithfulness go before you."* Righteousness is God's domain (Hebrew 1:8), God does no injustice (Zephaniah 3:5), God's righteousness is forever (2 Corinthians 9:9), God's righteousness is the ultimate standard of judgment (Acts 17:31) and, in His righteousness, He gives each according to his deeds (Romans 2:6).

MORAL

God is morally perfect (impeccable). God's perfection is expressed by several Hebrew words, one of which is *tamim*, which means "complete, sound, blameless, perfect and without blemish." *Shalem* is another Hebrew word for *perfect*, which means "complete, safe, blameless"; *tam* is also rendered "complete, blameless and perfect." The Greek word for *perfect* is *teleio*, which means "complete, perfect, mature"; *teleioo* bears the idea of "bringing to an end, completing, perfecting" (Geisler, 2011, p. 763). God is perfect in every way. Deuteronomy 32:4 (NIV) says, *"He is the Rock, his works are perfect, and all his ways are just. A faithful God who does no wrong, upright and just is He."*

OMNISCIENCE

God is perfect in His knowledge. Job 37:16 (NIV), *"Do you know how the clouds hang poised, those wonders of him who has perfect knowledge?"* The laws that God render are perfect. Psalm 19:7 (NIV), *"The law of the LORD is perfect, refreshing the soul. The statutes of the LORD are trustworthy, making wise the simple."* God fulfills His plans perfectly and faithfully. Psalm 138:8 (ESV), *"The LORD will fulfill his purpose for me;*

your steadfast love, O LORD, endures forever. Do not forsake the work of your hands."

IMMUTABLE

James chapter one reveals the attribute of immutability: *"Every good and perfect gift is from above, coming down from the Father of the heavenly lights, who does not change like shifting shadows"* (v. 17 NIV). God does not change because everything He does is perfect. If something is done perfectly, there is no need to change it. The more God is seen in His perfection, the more visible human imperfection becomes.

JEALOUS

Worshiping other gods provokes God's jealousy. *"Do not worship any other god, for the LORD, whose name is Jealous, is a jealous God"* (Exodus 34:14 NIV). Many may be surprised to know that God is jealous. The scripture declares jealousy as an essential characteristic of God by associating the characteristic with His identity.

God is jealous for what belongs to Him, and everything belongs to Him: *"The earth is the LORD's and the fullness thereof, the world and those who dwell therein"* (Psalm 24:1 ESV). The Hebrew word for *jealousy* is *kannaw*, which means "to be desirous of, to be zealous about, to be excited to anger over, to execute judgment because of, to desire earnestly and to be fervent" (Geisler, 2011, p. 764).

The primary Greek word for *jealousy* is *zeloo* which means, "to have strong affection toward, to be ardently devoted to, to desire earnestly, to be fervent." God's passionate jealousy can be seen in His opposition against idolatry in the following verse: *"You cannot drink the cup of the Lord and the cup of demons too; you cannot have a part in both the Lord's table and the table of demons. Are we trying to arouse the Lord's jealousy? Are we stronger than He?"* (1 Corinthians 10:21, 22 NIV). God's jealousy can be seen against idolatrous images in Psalm 78:58 (NKJV): *"For they provoked Him to anger with their high places, and moved Him to jealousy with their carved images."*

Sin stirs up the jealousy of God. 1 Kings 14:22 (ESV), *"And Judah did what was evil in the sight of the LORD, and they provoked him to jealousy with their sins that they committed, more than all that their fathers had done."*

God is jealous for His Holy name. Ezekiel 39:25 (ESV): *"Therefore thus says the Lord GOD: Now I will restore the fortunes of Jacob and have mercy on the whole house of Israel, and I will be jealous for my holy name."*

God is jealous for His holy people. Zechariah 8:2 (NIV): *"Thus says the LORD of hosts: I am jealous for Zion with great jealousy, and I am jealous for her with great wrath."*

God is jealous for His holy land (Joel 2:18) and His holy city (Zechariah 1:14). Avoiding God's jealous wrath means recognizing the fact that everything belongs to God, and He is to be honored and reverenced above all.

LOVE

God is love (1 John 4:16). The Hebrew word for *love* is *chesed*. When used in reference to God, it means "loving-kindness or tender loving-kindness." The Greek word for *love* is *agapé*. When used in reference to God, *agapé* means "selflessness or sacrificial" love (Geisler, 2011, p. 764).

God's love is everlastingly drawing, "*The LORD hath appeared of old unto me, saying, Yea, I have loved thee with an everlasting love: therefore with lovingkindness have I drawn thee*" (Jeremiah 31:1 KJV).

God rejoices over you. "*The LORD your God is in your midst, a mighty one who will save; he will rejoice over you with gladness; he will quiet you by his love; he will exult over you with loud singing*" (Zephaniah 3:17 ESV).

God's love has been poured into every believer's heart through the Holy Spirit because hope does not put to shame (Romans 5:5). "*For God so loved the world, that he gave his only Son, that whoever believes in him should not perish but have eternal life*" (John 3:16 ESV).

God's great love is referenced in Scriptures. "*But God, being rich in mercy, because of the great love with which he loved us, even when we were dead in our trespasses, made us alive together with Christ - by grace you have been saved*" (Ephesians 2:4 ESV).

God's love surpasses all understanding: "*and to know the love of Christ that surpasses knowledge, that you may be filled with all the fullness of God*" (Ephesians 3:19 NIV).

Believers are to walk in the same love. *"And walk in love, as Christ loved us and gave himself up for us, a fragrant offering and sacrifice to God"* (Ephesians 5:2, ESV).

The love that the Father has lavished onto us is incomprehensible, for we are called children of God (1 John 3:1). God's attributes do not infringe on other attributes as in parts; however, holiness is like the crown jewel. For example, God's love will not accept anything outside of what His grace has already provided. **The sinner cannot refuse Jesus (God's grace), and think that God's love will cover him from God's justice.**

TRUTH

God is truth, and nothing is false in Him. The Hebrew word for *truth* (*emeth*) means "firm, stable, faithful, reliable, correct." The Greek word for *truth* (*aletheia*) means "truthful, dependable, upright, real." Truth is taught in scripture as reality, and reality is dependable (Geisler, 2011, p. 765). Nothing is false in the truth. *"I write to you, not because you do not know the truth, but because you know it, and because no lie is of the truth"* (1 John 2:21 ESV).

God is eternal and has never lied. *"in hope of eternal life, which God, who never lies, promised before the ages began"*(Titus 1:2 ESV).

No lie comes from the truth; therefore, it is impossible for God to lie. *"So that by two unchangeable things, in which it is impossible for God to lie, we who have fled for refuge might have strong encouragement to hold fast to the hope set before us"* (Hebrew 6:18 ESV).

God distinguishes Himself from lying man. *"God is not man, that he should lie, or a son of man, that he should change his mind. Has he said, and will he not do it? Or has he spoken, and will he not fulfill it?* (Numbers 23:19 ESV).

God is absolute truth. *"God is the God of truth"* (Psalm 31:5 NASB). *"For the word of the LORD is upright, and all his work is done in faithfulness"* (Psalm 33:4 ESV).

Jesus identifies Himself as absolute truth in John 14:6 (NIV), which says, *"Jesus answered, "I am the way and the truth and the life. No one comes to the Father except through me."*

The Holy Spirit, the third person of the Trinity, is revealed as absolute truth as well. *"But when the Helper comes, whom I will send to you from the Father, the Spirit of truth, who proceeds from the Father, he will bear witness about me"* (John 15:26 ESV). This verse makes total logical sense for the Father, Son and Holy Spirit are one in essence and three in person.

God is called the living and true God in 1 Thessalonians 1:9 (ESV), which says, *"For they themselves report concerning us the kind of reception we had among you, and how you turned to God from idols to serve the living and true God."*

A characteristic of truth is truth listens to and obeys Truth. *"We are from God. Whoever knows God listens to us;*

whoever is not from God does not listen to us. By this we know the Spirit of truth and the spirit of error" (1 John 4:6 ESV). The believer can trust God's promises and be assured of His salvation (Psalm 89:35, 2 Timothy 2:13).

Part 3: Identity in Christ

How the Two Primary Sources of Sin Affect Identity

The first sin separated man from God and his true identity. God is the Source and Giver of life and identity. Even after redemption, sin can have an effect on the believer's relationship with God, others and identity (not to the extent of separation from God again!). This is evident in scripture for believers are told, *"Do not extinguish the Spirit"* (1 Thessalonians 5:19, New English Translation) and *"...do not grieve the Holy Spirit of God, by whom you were sealed for the day of redemption"* (Ephesians 4:30 ESV).

The two primary sources of sin are internal and external. *External sin* as the name implies is "outside the body." This sin is influenced by the world and the Devil (1 John 2:16). This category includes the world system with its empty philosophies, ideologies and demonic forces that are over the present darkness as referred to by the apostle Paul in the sixth chapter of Ephesians. External sin can be seen with the temptation of Eve in the garden and the temptation of Jesus in the wilderness (Matthew 4). External temptation is not only a challenge against God's authority but also His goodness.

External temptation can be seen in the media, on television, by means of the Internet and is often invoked by teachers and professors. External temptation is subtle and is often masked with a legitimate concern or desire. The Devil is a master at deceiving, twisting and misconstruing scripture, relationships and other good things that God has blessed man with for his benefit. The Devil makes good things appear less than good and more desirable outside of their intended bonds and purposes or he misleads man to believe that the good thing is better sooner.

Identity Called into Question with the First External Temptation

Eve's identity was ultimately questioned when the first question ever recorded in Scripture was asked. Eve had no reason to doubt God's goodness. After all, God had never wronged her. All she had ever known was His goodness. The Tempter, in his craftiness, questioned who Eve was in so many words and also informed her who she could become if she disobeyed the Word of God. This question made Eve question herself (her identity). The Devil knows that falsehood can be achieved by simply diverting a person from truth. No matter how insignificant or minor a diversion from truth may appear, it is still destructive, deadly and sets the course for all other decisions.

If the truth is distorted, what is left? A lie! For this reason, the Devil would promote (influence) the popular teaching of relativism, for the Devil wants people to believe anything but the truth. Believers should suspect that the Devil would say, "All truth is relative!" The person who believes this will be believing two lies; if he dodges one, he will be hit by the other. These lies are: 1) There are many "trues," and 2) Each person has his own truth.

In other words, are there no absolute laws in this universe? No! The law of biogenesis, which means that life always comes from life and life requires a specific chemistry for physical beings are powered by chemical reactions that are dependent on the laws of chemistry operating in a uniform fashion, is an absolute law (Lisle, 2006, Para. 4-5).

The Bible proclaims absolutes about all of life, yet the Word of God is not a science book. The Bible proclaims and teaches a specific message, and that message is either true or false, but cannot be both as the relativist proclaims. It cannot be said that the Bible, God's Word, is true along with other truths (other philosophies, ideologies) for the Bible claims to stand alone and says, *"Where is the wise person? Where is the teacher of the law? Where is the philosopher of this age? Has not God made foolish the wisdom of the world?"* (1 Corinthians 1:20 NIV).

Therefore, these two are not compatible. God says that He is the Truth, and He ALONE for the Devil has blinded and deceived the world (John 14:6, 2 Corinthians 4:4). A person cannot say that the Bible is true, and on the contrary, everything is relative. The Devil clearly does not want man to know the truth because the truth is productive, serves a God-intended purpose, builds up and sets captives free.

The Devil is fine with religion and the Bible to an extent. In fact, he may actually prefer religion and the Bible if he thinks doing so will lead more people astray. He loves hypocrisy and insincerity. "Go to church, just don't truly believe and practice the truth."

The aim of external temptation is to keep a person's mind and heart away from truth. The truth sets men free, and the Devil's goal is to keep men bound in sin. Relativism and similar philosophies are not setting people free because they are lies and not instructing people in the specific absolute truth of God's Word. These empty words lack the transforming power of God.

False and empty philosophies like these keep people bound for they teach lies, which lead people away from God, who is the ultimate absolute. God can be seen in the absolute sense when He "...*said to Moses, "I AM WHO I AM." And he said, "Say this to the people of Israel: 'I AM has sent me to you'"* (Exodus 3:14 ESV). This absolute is said to be the most famous verse in the Torah. *Relativism*, "the teaching of no absolutes," robs people from the possibility of arriving at the truth.

Scripture teaches man not to swerve to the right or to the left (Proverbs 4:27). Today's philosophies, on the other hand, teach that there is no actual right or left to swerve to or from. Jesus constantly spoke of Himself, the kingdom of God, heaven, earth and everything else in the absolute sense. Jesus said, *"Enter by the narrow gate. For the gate is wide and the way is easy that leads to destruction, and those who enter by it are many"* (Matthew 7:13 ESV). Jesus also says plainly, *"...I am the way, and the truth, and the life. No one comes to the Father except through me"* (John 14:6 ESV).

The relativists who frequently teach their heresies in today's schools and culture propose there is no universal right, wrong or purpose, and therefore, no identity can be sought for each individual; rather, identity is relative. There can be no absolute gate into which to enter the relativist says; rather, the seeker chooses which one of many gates fits him. Sometimes the gates lead in different directions; at other times, they all face the same way. Philosophies have implications; they are not simply words or sayings. Identity is real; every being has an identity.

IDENTITY IN THE MIDST OF A STORM

When identity is established, let no man doubt his identity. If God reveals and commands, He will provide the means to carry out what He has commanded. Scripture shows Jesus' commanding Peter to walk on the water to come to Him. Before this incident, the reader can assume that Peter had never walked on water, but at that moment, based on the command of God, Peter believed and acted on his belief. Peter was fine focusing on Savior until the storm came. He was fine until he took his eyes off the Savior. When he took his eyes off Jesus and focused on the conditions of the storm, he started to sink. The storm was true; it did exist. However, the storm was under the control of the One who commanded him to come. In other words, when the believer takes his eyes off of Jesus, the believer beginnings to sink.

When God tells man who he is and commands things of him, man is given the wherewithal to perform them. In Peter's case (and every believer's), the storm is only a test. Yes, the storm is real; however, God sends the storm to strengthen the believer. James writes, *"because you know that the testing of your faith produces perseverance"* (James 1:3 NIV).

Likewise, Jesus encourages believers not to be afraid of temporal things like trials and tribulations but rather only to fear him who can destroy the body and the soul (Matthew 10:28). Often believers forget this essential principle when trials come and losing their focus, they sink, forgetting that their identity is found in Jesus, the Potter, who painstakingly fashions their trials to mold them into His likeness (Isaiah 64:8).

To avoid losing focus, the believer has to make it a priority not to become entangled in human desires, but rather to meditate on the Words of the Lord day and night (Psalm 1:2). The apostle Paul writes similarly to Timothy: *"No soldier gets entangled in civilian pursuits, since his aim is to please the one who enlisted him"* (2 Timothy 2:4 ESV).

The Tempter is crafty. He asked Eve a question and allowed her to fill in the blank. As Eve was walking in the truth and in fellowship with God, the Tempter came with a question that was asked with the intent to question God's goodness and man's freedom. The Tempter encouraged Eve to focus on the temporal: feelings, esteem, etc. and not on truth, consequences and the death that had been promised for disobedience.

The Enemy only wanted Eve to consider that her perception was correct: God was not totally good, her ideas were right and could be used to measure God or she could disobey God and good would come of her disobedience.

In other words, the Devil deceived Eve into thinking that she had more power than she truly did. The Enemy precipitated Eve's deceptive thoughts which were not cast down; therefore, they took root. The believer is commanded to cast down every thought, imagination, ideology and argument that rises up against the knowledge of God. The believer is also instructed not to entertain or ponder contrary thoughts, but rather, to bring them captive to the obedience of Christ (2 Corinthians 10:5).

Bringing thoughts into captivity takes a mindset that is not focused on the temporal or the fleshly:

"For if you live according to the flesh you will die, but if by the Spirit you put to death the deeds of the body, you will live" (Romans 8:13 ESV).

> "*For to set the mind on the flesh is death, but to set the mind on the Spirit is life and peace*" (Romans 8:6 ESV).
>
> "*For the wages of sin is death, but the free gift of God is eternal life in Christ Jesus our Lord*" (Romans 6:23 ESV).

The Devil painted a deceitful picture that God was unjust to withhold something from His creature and was therefore not good. If God was indeed withholding something good from Eve, she had the right and the means to correct this wrong. Temptation had something desirable to offer Eve. The bait for Eve was increasing in knowledge; the hook was the perceived means of obtaining this desire. Eve knew the truth, and she should have protected it. Had she resisted the Devil, he would have fled (James 4:6, 7; Matthew 13:20).

Desire must be distinguished from *identity*. The strong wanting or wishing that comes with a desire is not unacceptable; however, the Spirit must control the desire for the believer's true identity is found in Christ. Since man's identity is found in Christ, "*...walk by the Spirit, and you will not gratify the desires of the flesh*" (Galatians 5:16 NIV), consequently, the believer should "*Put to death, therefore, whatever belongs to your earthly nature: sexual immorality, impurity, lust, evil desires and greed, which is idolatry*" (Colossians 3:5 NIV).

Identity is truly recognized when a person trusts God enough to entrust Him with all. This commitment is not asking too much for Romans deems this to be the believer's reasonable service (12:2). The one who does not trust God in the Spirit is in the flesh where there is no peace (Romans 8:6). Therefore, he will forever be seeking identity and never obtaining that for which he searches. That person is like the unsettled men about whom Paul wrote a warning to Timothy: *"always learning and never able to arrive at a knowledge of the truth"* (2 Timothy 3:7 ESV).

The person who walks in the flesh will be controlled by the flesh, trapped desiring a peace that only God can provide. Again, *"For in him we live and move and have our being* [identity]" (Acts 17:28 ESV).

The truth must be known in order to be lived. *"How, then, can they call on the one they have not believed in? And how can they believe in the one of whom they have not heard? And how can they hear without someone preaching to them?"* (Romans 10:14 NIV).

The Effects of Internal Sin on Identity

The second source of sin is *internal*, which James refers to as *"evil desire"* (1:14). The world, the Devil and the demons are external tempters, provokers. Internal sin, on the other hand, is the evil desires that come from within. Before sin (or temptation) is presented, a person has to determine to yield or refuse it. Satan's goal is to kill, steal and destroy, and the best way he can accomplish his modus operandi is through deception and keeping a person from the Truth

(Jesus and His Word). The person with no truth will surely fall to death and destruction.

No one is immune to temptation. James portrays temptation as a fisherman luring in his catch with bait before he is hooked. Paul, like James, doesn't allow believers to deceive themselves. When he speaks of "another law" at work within him, he is referring to a "law" that prompts him toward sin and evil (Romans 7:21-24).

Believers are called to walk by the Spirit so they will not gratify the desires of the flesh; after all, the two are opposed to one another (Galatians 5:16, 17). In these verses, the apostle is calling God's people to continue habitually in the Spirit of God as a lifestyle. This is part of the Holy Spirit's work as Sanctifier. These verses also present the idea that the believer is to continuously submit to the leading or control of the Spirit. This deference to His leading is a progression in godliness. Living in the Spirit is submission of the will, mind and emotions.

This submission of the will, mind and emotions can be seen in what the apostle Peter wrote to the church:

> *Therefore, preparing your minds for action, and being sober-minded, set your hope fully on the grace that will be brought to you at the revelation of Jesus Christ. As obedient children, do not be conformed to the passions of your former ignorance, but as he who called you is holy, you also be holy in all your conduct, since it is written, "You shall be holy, for I am holy"* (1 Peter 1:13-16 ESV).

The term *saint* means "one who is holy"; however, a person is not holy in and of himself. Rather, that person must rely on the Holy Spirit to accomplish this work. Internal temptation (fleshly desire) remains forever present, and the apostle Paul offers some sound advice: *"But I discipline my body and keep it under control, lest after preaching to others I myself should be disqualified"* (1 Corinthians 9:27 ESV).

Believers are mandated to submit to the Holy Spirit and not let sin reign in their mortal bodies so that they obey its evil desires. Believers are commanded not to offer any part of themselves to sin as instruments of wickedness, but rather to offer themselves to God as instruments of righteousness. Jesus has brought the believer from death to life, and sin no longer has rule over him because he is no longer under the law, but under grace (Romans 6:12-14).

Discontentment Is a Result of sin

A believer's failing to understand his identity in Christ will lead to discontentment and discontentment is the result of sin. As the believer tries to take every thought captive and make them obedient to the knowledge of Christ, he often realizes that his thoughts are covetous, which emanates from a discontented heart (2 Corinthians 10:5). Paul told Timothy that godliness with contentment was great gain (1 Timothy 6:6). The Christian's duty is to be content and immovable in all circumstances, knowing that all of their needs are met in Christ.

Christians are warned to maintain their continency.

"for we brought nothing into the world, and we cannot take anything out of the world. But if we have food and clothing, with these we will be content. But those who desire to be rich fall into temptation, into a snare, into many senseless and harmful desires that plunge people into ruin and destruction" (1 Timothy 6:7-9 ESV).

Likewise, Christians are instructed not to be anxious like unbelievers, but to be content because their Heavenly Father knows their needs. However, this command is not to be viewed as a passive command for the scripture does not stop there, but rather instructs the believer to actively *"seek first the kingdom of God and his righteousness, and all these things will be added to you"* (Matthew 6:33 ESV).

Seeking the kingdom of God is the highest priority, the supreme goal for the believer. The believer is affirmed over and over again throughout scripture and should be confident that God will meet all of his needs (Matthew 16:25, 10:39). When the believer seeks first the kingdom of God, he expresses faith and trust in God, thus allowing His will to be done and not trying to move the hand of God or work things out for himself (in the flesh). Walking in the flesh is death, but walking in the Spirit is life (Romans 8:6, 7).

On the contrary, all that God does not supply is not to be looked at as a negative, but as an action that is according to His perfect wisdom and ultimate plan. The believer will be able to say, like Paul, that God's grace is sufficient (2 Corinthians 12:9).

True contentment relates to the Christian's understanding of God, His sovereignty and grace. The apostle says that he learned the secret of having plenty and being in need (Philippians 4:12). The secret is the Christian's position in Christ. The apostle Paul understood his place in Christ. While applying and practicing his faith, the apostle Paul grew in faith and understanding, knowing that all things worked for his good (Romans 8:28), bringing him to the point of being content in every situation (sanctification). Hence, believers are to be careful in how they live, making good use of their time, being wise and not foolish, and understanding what the will of the Lord is (Ephesians 5:15-17).

THE DISCONTENTMENT OF THE FLESH

The flesh leads into temptation, snares, and many other foolish and harmful desires, which plunge people into destruction and ruin (1 Timothy 6:9, 10). That man who gives into fleshly desires will be discontent because the flesh is never satisfied. Solomon addressed this discontentment when he penned the following verse: *"Death and Destruction are never satisfied, and neither are human eyes"* (Proverb 27:20 NIV). Human eyes, the flesh and its desires are never satisfied. For this reason the Christian is told over and over again to deny and crucify the flesh daily (Matthew 16:24, Mark 8:34, Romans 6:6, Galatians 5:24).

In his first letter to the church, Peter explained denying self like this: *"Beloved, I urge you as sojourners and exiles to abstain from the passions of the flesh, which wage war against your soul."* (2:11 ESV). Peter describes the believer as a sojourner, a foreigner or an alien, referring to his relationship to this world, emphasizing the fact that the believer is only passing through. John described the world as a place of lust and pride. *"For everything in the world—the lust of the flesh, the lust of the eyes, and the pride of life—comes not from the Father but from the world"* (1 John 2:16 NIV).

Sin is deceitful, and if one is cherished, that sin will hinder the believer from having fellowship with God (1 Corinthians 11:30, 1 John 5:16). In order to be content and sure of his identity, the believer must live (walk) in the identity (the Spirit). Living and walking in the Spirit refers to, but is not limited to, a continual intentional daily activity. So as a believer obediently walks in the Spirit, he will grow in the Lord, casting down more and more thoughts that rise up against the knowledge of God (Galatians 5:25, 2 Corinthians 10:5). That believer thus prevents evil thoughts from having an effect on his contentment and identity in Christ.

UNDERSTANDING SIN TO UNDERSTAND HOW SIN AFFECTS MAN'S IDENTITY
THE ORIGIN OF SIN

Sin was present in the garden before the sin of Adam and Eve. Sin before the fall is recorded in the book of Isaiah:

"How art thou fallen from heaven, O Lucifer, son of the morning! how art thou cut down to the ground, which didst weaken the nations! For thou hast said in thine heart, I will ascend into heaven, I will exalt my throne above the stars of God: I will sit also upon the mount of the congregation, in the sides of the north: I will ascend above the heights of the clouds; I will be like the most High" (Isaiah 14:12-14 NKJV).

Sin not only exists because God has created mankind to choose, but also because He is patient, full of grace and merciful. Some modern liberal scholars have tried to minimize, dull and/or pass off sin as simply a hindrance that possesses the possibility, if bad enough, to affect a person's esteem or identity. The Bible, on the other hand, says that sin is so wicked and evil that it will affect beings on into eternity. The eternal effects of sin can be seen in Isaiah and John's prophecies. *"Let the one who does wrong continue to do wrong; let the vile person continue to be vile; let the one who does right continue to do right; and let the holy person continue to be holy"* (Revelation 22:11 NIV).

"And they shall go out and look on the dead bodies of the men who have rebelled against me. For their worm shall not die, their fire shall not be quenched, and they shall be an abhorrence to all flesh" (Isaiah 66:24 ESV).

God did not create or cause sin. Both Ezekiel (28:12-18) and Isaiah describe the origin of sin as starting with the narcissistic thoughts of Satan:

How you have fallen from heaven, morning star, son of the dawn! You have been cast down to the earth, you who once laid low the nations! You said in your heart, "I will ascend to the heavens; I will raise my throne above the stars of God; I will sit enthroned on the mount of assembly, on the utmost heights of Mount Zaphon. I will ascend above the tops of the clouds; I will make myself like the Most High" (Isaiah 14:12-14 NIV).

The apostle Paul in 1 Timothy 3:6 interprets these scriptures literally when he said that a man must not be a recent convert or he may become conceited and fall under the same judgment as the Devil (1 Timothy 3:6). The Holy Spirit (God) is the Author of the Bible, and He used Paul (among others) to record His words. If the Holy Spirit interprets these verses in a literal way, who are modern-day scholars not to do likewise?

SIN ON EARTH

Man was created as a free, volitional being. In this freedom, he was in a original state of sinless perfection, not only innocent and without sin, but also in a state of righteousness. This state consisted of a nature inclined to love and do good rather than evil. Scripture teaches that man was not in a state of equilibrium with the ability to choose wrong as easily as choosing right; rather, he was naturally prone toward the good and holy. Man, nonetheless, was still only a mere created being. The excellence that man naturally held was bestowed and was not essential or inalienable.

The enticement to do wrong started with a question of impartiality: *"For God knows that when you eat from it your eyes will be opened, and you will be like God, knowing good and evil"* (Genesis 3:5 NIV). The question was intended to cause doubt and/or entice the listener by the temptation of increasing in existence, knowledge and/or gratification.

God is continuously seen in scripture as the ultimate authority:

> *The LORD God took the man and put him into the garden of Eden to work it and keep it. And the LORD God commanded the man, saying, "You may surely eat of every tree of the garden, but of the tree of the knowledge of good and evil you shall not eat, for in the day that you eat of it you shall surely die"* (Genesis 2:15-17 ESV).

God declared everything He created to be good; man was adequate, whole and complete in his identity. Man's duty was to obey, cultivate and keep what God had entrusted to him. In verses 16 and 17 of chapter two, Adam was given permission to eat from any tree except the tree of the knowledge of good and evil. In these scriptures, the Creator and Purpose Giver can be seen rendering guidelines to His creatures. Adam's actions and decisions then were to fall into the guidelines and commands given by the ultimate Authority and Owner.

Perfect identity was turned into imperfection with one act of disobedience. This one act plunged mankind into confusion. The narrative of this event starts with a question and ends with Adam's disobeying his Creator by eating the forbidden fruit. Clearly, God did not sin nor did He tempt anyone to sin (James 1:13); man sinned by his own act of volition.

To say that God sinned or had anything to do with sin in any way is blasphemy. Sin started with choice, and with that choice came consequences. The two major consequence of sin were alienation and corruption; with these consequences, identity was confused with an inclination (enslavement) to sin rather than to do right.

ALIENATION EQUALS IDENTITY CONFUSION
With the first sin, a cosmic change took place. Man's relationship to God, creation, himself and to others changed. This "change in relationship" is often referred to as *separation, alienation* or *estrangement*.

Man is saved and justified before God the moment he believes in Jesus; he is said to be *reconciled* unto God:

"Therefore, since we have been justified through faith, we have peace with God through our Lord Jesus Christ" (Romans 5:1 NIV).

> *"All this is from God, who reconciled us to himself through Christ and gave us the ministry of reconciliation"* (2 Corinthians 5:18 NIV).

Reconciliation is only necessary when a separation has taken place.

First, a separation occurs between man and God. The fact that man is naturally in a state of opposition to God can be seen in Romans chapter 8, which says, *"The mind governed by the flesh is hostile to God; it does not submit to God's law, nor can it do so"* (v. 7 NIV).

The flesh, however, does not govern believers. In today's culture, people are quick to say that God loves them unconditionally; however, they willingly ignore the separation that sin has caused. God is love, but at the same time, He is just and righteous. A person can be punished out of love. In fact, the Bible is dedicated to showing man step-by-step the provision God has made for him and why he needs the provision. The provision is the Gospel (good news) and man is commanded to believe and obey in order to escape the wrath to come (God's judgment). However, people in ignorance and unbelief often think and convince themselves that God will accept less than perfect, as though they are doing God a favor! They tend to forget that He said, *"All of us have become like one who is unclean, and all our righteous acts are like filthy rags; we all shrivel up like a leaf, and like the wind our sins sweep us away"* (Isaiah 64:6 NIV).

God has made His terms clear. *"How shall we escape if we ignore so great a salvation?"* (Hebrews 2:3, NIV). Through grace men receive revelation from God, and with revelation comes instruction, purpose and identity. The Lord says to whom much is given, much is required (Luke 12:48). What will be the punishment for those who ignore such clear and compelling revelation? What will be the result of those who willfully turn away from what they know to be true and right?

Jesus told His disciples in Matthew 10:15 that it will be more bearable on the day of judgment for the land of Sodom and Gomorrah than for the cities that reject His Word. The goal of salvation is to reconcile two parties, and if the two parties are not reconciled, they will forever be estranged (separated). This lack of reconciliation means no Heaven for the estranged because debts must be paid. Sinners who choose to reject Christ must pay their own debt in Hell.

Secondly, sin not only affected humans, it affected the entire earth. A description of the effects of sin can be seen in Romans chapter 8, which says, *"For we know that the whole creation has been groaning together in the pains of childbirth until now. And not only the creation, but we ourselves, who have the first fruits of the Spirit, groan inwardly as we wait eagerly for adoption as sons, the redemption of our bodies"* (vv. 22, 23 ESV).

Creation was affected negatively, for when Adam fell, everything within his domain also fell because God had given him dominion over "*...the fish of the sea and over the birds of the heavens and over every living thing that moves on the earth*" (Genesis 1:28 ESV). God cursed the ground after the fall, making it resistant to the hands of fallen man (Sproul, 2014, p. 104).

Thirdly, man is alienated from one another, not only on the individual level with violence against one's neighbor, but also on the global level with nations rising up against nations (Mark 13:8). When man sins, it is first a sin against God then against one's neighbor. Man harms and attempts to bring harm to his neighbor from the failure to recognize a common identity, which is a result of separation (Sproul, 2014, p. 104).

Fourth, man is alienated from himself. At the core, many people are not satisfied with themselves. As a result, man attempts to combat this problem of this self-alienation by keeping God out and focusing on self-esteem and human dignity (Sproul, 2014, p. 104). Man again tries to be God rather than humbling himself and listening to Him. Often, when man attempts to protect his self-esteem, self-worth and dignity, the next person matters little.

Self-fulfillment seems to be one of the primary objectives in the current culture, yet those seeking it only discover more discontentment. Man becomes more self-centered and more depressed after he has exhausted himself in pursuit of himself. He is naturally self-seeking (selfish), and therefore, needs to explore outside of himself. The self-esteem movement proves that man has a self-esteem problem, and the solution cannot involve more of the problem. Man does not have to be taught or encouraged to seek himself because this is the core of the problem (Sproul, 2014, p. 104).

Fifth, an alienation from labor occurs. In every type of vocation, human beings have some form of pain or struggle. Work was intended to bring glory to God and fulfillment to man. The change in this relationship can be traced back to the garden where the curse of God came upon man's work. Labor itself is not cursed. Before the curse, man was put on earth to work. After creating the world and the universe, God rested and blessed the seventh day (Sproul, 2014, p. 104). God's six days of work was the original intent for man as well.

SIN SEPARATES MANKIND FROM THE SOURCE OF IDENTITY

"It's your sins that have cut you off from God. Because of your sins, he has turned away and will not listen anymore" (Isaiah 59:2 New Living Translation).

Adam is often referred to as the federal head of mankind for his actions as the elect representative affected all of mankind. After eating the forbidden fruit, mankind's nature was changed. According to the following scriptures, Adam was the root of mankind:

"For as in Adam all die, so in Christ all will be made alive" (1 Corinthians 15:22 NIV).

> *"Nevertheless, death reigned from the time of Adam to the time of Moses, even over those who did not sin by breaking a command, as did Adam, who is a pattern of the one to come."* (Romans 5:14 NIV).

Genesis 6:5 (NIV): *"The LORD saw how great the wickedness of the human race had become on the earth, and that every inclination of the thoughts of the human heart was only evil all the time."* The phrase, *"...the human race had become,"* illustrates that it had not always been that way. The guilt and corruption of Adam has been imputed to all of mankind, for all of mankind sin. This imputation should be viewed like the righteousness that is imputed onto believers by Jesus when believers believe.

SEPARATION VIEWED BY THE EARLY CHURCH

The saints at Westminster and at London both agreed on the following:

I. Our first parents, being seduced by the subtilty and temptations of Satan, sinned, in eating the forbidden fruit. This their sin, God was pleased, according to His wise and holy counsel, to permit, having purposed to order it to His own glory.

II. By this sin they fell from their original righteousness and communion, with God, and so became dead in sin, and wholly defiled in all the parts and faculties of soul and body.

III. They being the root of all mankind, the guilt of this sin was imputed; and the same death in sin, and corrupted nature, conveyed to all their posterity descending from them by ordinary generation.

IV. From this original corruption, whereby we are utterly indisposed, disabled, and made opposite to all good, and wholly inclined to all evil, do proceed all actual transgressions (*The Westminster Confession*, 2017, Chapter VI.I-IV; *The Baptist Confession*, 1689, Chapter 6.1-4).

The Source

With Jesus identified as the source, the believer is instructed not to worry about anything for if God clothes the grass of the field and feeds the birds of the sky, He will surely care for His children (Matthew 6:26, 31). God knows all needs and desires and is not so distant that He cannot hear or understand.

Jesus is not only the source for earthly and temporal things, however, for according to the following passages, He is the source of the believer's identity:

* *And in Christ you have been brought to fullness. He is the head over every power and authority* (Colossians 2:10 NIV).

* *But whoever is united with the Lord is one with him in spirit* (1 Corinthians 6:17 NIV).

- *Now you are the body of Christ, and each one of you is a part of it* (1 Corinthians 12:27 NIV).
- *For you died, and your life is now hidden with Christ in God* (Colossians 3:3 NIV).

With the believer's identity found in Christ, how does it look? The apostle Paul tells believers in Romans 12:1, 2 (ESV):

> "*I appeal to you therefore, brothers, by the mercies of God, to present your bodies as a living sacrifice, holy and acceptable to God, which is your spiritual worship. Do not be conformed to this world, but be transformed by the renewal of your mind, that by testing you may discern what is the will of God, what is good and acceptable and perfect.*"

Since all things are for His glory, the believer must respond by offering himself for the fulfillment of God's purpose. The believer accomplishes this by presenting his body as a living sacrifice. Under the Old Covenant, an acceptable sacrifice was a dead animal, but because of Jesus' sacrifice, the Old Testament sacrificial system of dead animals is no longer of any effect (Hebrews 9:11, 12).

The worship for those in Christ to offer is self in sacrificial worship. The basic element of worship is obedience (1 Samuel 15:22, Mark 12:30). That person must do more than simply offer himself as a sacrificial offering however; he must do so with true sincerity. The Old Testament prophets denounced the people of Israel for failing to be sincere. They instructed that God would only accept gifts that came from a pure heart:

"For I desire steadfast love and not sacrifice, the knowledge of God rather than burnt offerings" (Hosea 6:6 ESV).

Not simply a profession of love, but rather the type of love that Jesus taught: *"Whoever has my commandments and keeps them, he it is who loves me. And he who loves me will be loved by my Father, and I will love him and manifest myself to him."* (John 14:21 ESV)

"To love him with all your heart, with all your understanding and with all your strength, and to love your neighbor as yourself is more important than all burnt offerings and sacrifices" (Mark 12:33 NIV).

"Not for your sacrifices do I rebuke you; your burnt offerings are continually before me" (Psalm 50:8 ESV).

"To do righteousness and justice is more acceptable to the LORD than sacrifice" (Proverbs 21:3 ESV).

That the highest sacrificial service is owed to God only makes sense, for man enjoys the fruit of God's mercies every day. This theology is practical like all theology and is meant to be practiced (lived out). The theology of the Gospel of Jesus Christ is intended to transform lives, and until this theology is understood and lived out, it has not accomplished its purpose. The sacrifice offered up to God is not to be offered up ignorantly like the dead animals who were led to the slaughter; rather, the believer is to be well-informed and willing to offer himself intelligently.

The renewed mind comes into play at this point (the second verse in Paul's teaching Romans 12:2). The mind is renewed by constant study, meditation and practice of the truth of God. The renewed mind is, therefore, to be saturated and controlled by the Word of God.

One great temptation in the life of the Christian is to divide or separate the spiritual life from the physical, material life. The believer who thinks in this way gives eternal significance to only certain parts of his life; for identity to be considered in this way is dangerous. For the worship that God expects is sincere and continuous.

SINCERITY OR ASSURANCE?

King Solomon sums up the duty of man: "Now all has been heard; here is the conclusion of the matter: Fear God and keep his commandments, for this is the duty of all mankind." (Ecclesiastes 12:13 NIV). Never give men false assurance. The person who doubts his relationship to the Lord could have good reason. Some have confused sincerity in assurance with justification while disregarding the call to assess, test and examine his life and doctrine

(1 Timothy 4:16, 2 Corinthians 13:5). The call for examination is not for the immature and/or new believer alone. The Holy Spirit convicts of sin and is working to sanctify all those who are in Christ Jesus.

The believer's confidence should not be in the knowledge of Jesus; rather, his confidence should be in Jesus. Right and true knowledge is imperative, but the believer is not to put his faith and hope in knowledge, but rather in the person of Jesus Christ ALONE. When a person truly understands God's holy and unachievable standards, he realizes that he can do nothing but look to God for salvation.

Doubting could be a good sign that a problem exists. Assurance should not be stressed to the point of false assurance. True assurance comes when the person is sure. An individual is convinced and sure through the work of the Holy Spirit and by looking at his life. Paul writes empowered by the Holy Spirit:

> *"For you did not receive the spirit of slavery to fall back into fear, but you have received the Spirit of adoption as sons, by whom we cry, "Abba! Father!" The Spirit himself bears witness with our spirit that we are children of God, and if children, then heirs—heirs of God and fellow heirs with Christ, provided we suffer with him in order that we may also be glorified with him"* (Romans 8:15-17 ESV).

Jesus said the following in relation to genuine believers and character:

> *"Beware of false prophets, who come to you in sheep's clothing but inwardly are ravenous wolves. You will recognize them by their fruits. Are grapes gathered from thornbushes, or figs from thistles? So, every healthy tree bears good fruit, but the diseased tree bears bad fruit"* (Matthew 7:15-17 ESV).

Therefore, in spite of a person's seemingly orthodox theology, his fruit confirms the truth. The only way to know is to let the person's fruit speak for itself.

The world has clear, identifiable characteristics, and so does the Christian. Paul had no problem warning believers to be armed for battle against the schemes of the Devil (Ephesians 6:10-18). One essential tool for battle is the ability to discern worldly wisdom from Godly wisdom (1 Corinthians 1:20-31). Clear vision is imperative; the believer lives in a physical world but does not handle his problems as the world handles theirs (2 Corinthians 10:3).

In today's culture, drawing a clear distinction between the church and the world is not a simple task for many "churches" have adapted the world's ways and philosophies. Believers are warned in the first letter to Timothy that, in the later times, some will depart from the faith by devoting themselves to deceitful spirits and teachings of demons, and people will not put up with or tolerate sound doctrine (teaching). Rather, they will gather teachers who will suit or tell them what they desire to hear (1 Timothy 4:1, 2 Timothy 4:3). The Believer cannot and should not sit in an environment where the Word of God is not preached and taught (Jude 1:4, 2 Peter 2:1, 1 Timothy 2:14).

Nevertheless Believers are not to try to identify or pluck out weeds:

> *"But he* [Jesus] *said, 'No, lest in gathering the weeds you root up the wheat along with them. Let both grow together until the harvest, and at harvest time I will tell the reapers, 'Gather the weeds first and bind them in bundles to be burned, but gather the wheat into my barn'"* (Matthew 13:29, 30 ESV).

THE IDENTITY OF THE ENEMY

The character of the Enemy has not changed. He is still telling believers the same thing he told Eve. During Eve's temptation, she saw that the forbidden tree was desirable and good for food. The fruit was a delight to the eye and desirable to make a person wise, so she took of its fruit and ate, giving some to her husband (Genesis 3:6).

Satan appealed to Eve's desire for food (lust of the flesh). Eve's desire for something delightful to the eye, attractive (lust of the eyes), and her desire to have wisdom (pride of life).

The Three-pronged Attack on Eve

The same exact scheme was attempted on the second Adam (Jesus). However, Satan appealed to Jesus much more robustly. He appealed first to Jesus' human desire for food, knowing that Jesus had not eaten for forty days (lust of flesh), he showed Jesus the attractiveness of the kingdoms of the world (lust of the eyes), and he attempted to provoke Jesus to be prideful by telling Him to throw Himself down to prove He was the Son of God (pride of life).

The Devil, the believer's greatest external Enemy is an opportunist, and the believer is warned and called to be ready and sober-minded: *"Be sober-minded; be watchful. Your adversary the devil prowls around like a roaring lion, seeking someone to devour"* (1 Peter 5:8 ESV).

In 1521, Martin Luther declared the following at the Diet of Worms:

> Unless I am convinced by Scripture and plain reason—I do not accept the authority of the popes and councils, for they have contradicted each other—my conscience is captive to the Word of God. I cannot and I will not recant anything for to go against conscience is neither right nor safe. God help me. Amen.

WORKS CITED

Allison, G. R. (2011). *Historical Theology: An Introduction to Christian Doctrine*. Grand Rapids: Zondervan.

Ancestry.com LLC Reports Fourth Quarter and Full Year 2015 Financial Results. (2016). Retrieved from http://www.ancestry.com/corporate/newsroom/press-releases/ancestrycom-llc-reports-fourth-quarter-and-full-year-2015-financial-results.

Biblica, Inc. (2011). *New International Version*. Grand Rapids: Zondervan.

Conditional Sentences—Rules You Need to Know. (2017). Retrieved from https://www.grammarly.com/blog/conditional-sentences/.

Edwards, J. (2011). *Freedom of the Will*. Lexington: Legacy Publications.

Geisler, N. L. (1977). *A Popular Survey of the Old Testament*. Grand Rapids: Baker Academics.

_____. (2011). *Systematic Theology in One Volume*. Minneapolis: Bethany House.

Gilson, E., & Shook, L. (1994). *The Christian Philosophy of St. Thomas Aquinas*. New York: Random House, Inc.

God Glorified in Man's Dependence. (1731). Retrieved from http://www.jonathan-edwards.org/Dependence.html.

Grudem, W. (1994). *Systematic Theology*. Grand Rapids: Zondervan.

The Holy Bible, English Standard Version. ESV® Permanent Text Edition® (2016). Copyright © 2001 by Crossway Bibles, a publishing ministry of Good News Publishers.

The Holy Bible, King James Version (KJV), Public Domain.

The Holy Bible, New American Standard Bible (NASB), Copyright © 1960, 1962, 1963, 1968, 1971, 1972, 1973, 1975, 1977, 1995 by The Lockman Foundation.

The Holy Bible, New English Translation (NET), NET Bible® copyright ©1996-2006 by Biblical Studies Press, L.L.C. http://netbible.com. All rights reserved.

The Holy Bible, New International Version®, NIV® Copyright ©1973, 1978, 1984, 2011 by Biblica, Inc.® Used by permission. All rights reserved worldwide.

The Holy Bible, New King James Version (NKJV). Scripture taken from the New King James Version®.

Copyright © 1982 by Thomas Nelson. Used by permission. All rights reserved.

The Holy Bible, New Living Translation, copyright © 1996, 2004, 2015 by Tyndale House Foundation. Used by permission of Tyndale House Publishers Inc., Carol Stream, Illinois 60188. All rights reserved.

Howell, Dr. R. T. (2014). What Causes Materialism in America? . Retrieved from https://www.psychology today.com/blog/cant-buy-happiness/201403/what-causes-materialism-in-america.

"How should a Christian view materialism?". (2017). Retrieved from https://www.gotquestions.org/materialism-Christian.html.

Identity. (2017). Retrieved from http://www.dictionary.com/browse/identity.

Lisle, Dr. J. (2006). God & Natural Law. Retrieved from https://answersingenesis.org/is-god-real/god-natural-law/.

London Baptist Confession of 1689. (2017). Retrieved from http://www.theopedia.com/london-baptist-confession-of-1689.

Luther at the Imperial Diet of Worms (1521). (1997). Retrieved from http://www.luther.de/en/worms.html.

MacArthur, J. (1997). *MacArthur Study Bible (NKJV)*. Nashville: Thomas Nelson.

_____. (1997). *The John MacArthur Study Bible* [Peer commentary on the book by J. MacArthur].

Mayhon, A. M. (2016, June 17, 2016). How to Preach Biblically "Summary." *John MacArthur.*

Moo, D. J. (1996). *The Epistle to the Romans.* Grand Rapids: Wm. B. Eerdmans Publishing Co.

O'Brien, P. T. (1999). *The Letter to the Ephesians.* Grand Rapids: Wm. B. Eerdmans Publishing Co.

Owen, J. (2013 reprint). *The Death of Death in the Death of Christ.* East Peoria, IL: The Banner of Truth Trust.

Packer, J. (1990). *A Quest For Godliness: The Puritan Vision of Christian Life.* Crossway Books: a Division of Good News Publishers.

Sproul, R. (2005). *The Reformation Study Bible (ESV).* Lake Mary, FL: Ligonier Ministries.

_____. (2011). *The Reformation Study Bible* [Peer commentary on the book "Holy Bible" by R. Sproul].

_____. (2014). *Everyone's a Theologian: An Introduction to Systematic Theology*. Sanford, FL: Reformation Trust Publishing.

Spurgeon, C. H. (2011). *The Soul Winner*. Plymouth, Michigan: Legacy Publishing.

Stewart, H. (2010). Consumer Spending and the Economy. Retrieved from https://fivethirty eight.blogs.nytimes.com/2010/09/19/consumer-spending-and-the-economy/?_r=0.

The Baptist Confession of Faith. (1689). Retrieved from http://www.vor.org/truth/1689/1689bc00.html.

The Westminster Confession of Faith. (2017). Retrieved from http://www.reformed.org/documents/wcf_with_proofs/.

"What is the Westminster Confession of Faith?" (2017). Retrieved from https://www.gotquestions.org/Westminster-Confession-of-Faith.html.